Praise for *By Life or by Death*

By Life or by Death is a beautifully written and updated account of an inspiring missionary story well known to a previous generation. This powerful story, which presents a clear picture of two lives fully surrendered to Christ, will prompt readers who reflect on this moving story to join together to give thanks to God for the global influence and faithful service of John and Betty Stam as they faced martyrdom for the sake of the kingdom of Christ. Congratulations are in order for Andrew Montonera on providing this fine biography, which I am delighted to recommend for a new generation of readers.

David S. Dockery
President, International Alliance for Christian Education
President, Southwestern Baptist Theological Seminary, Fort Worth, Texas

My mother, Elisabeth Elliot, was profoundly influenced by John and Betty Stam's unwavering commitment to take the good news of Jesus Christ to China in spite of the danger. Communism was taking over the country. Mother's own obedience to Christ began to take shape at a very young age and solidified when she learned of the Stams' tragic deaths. Their martyrdom impacted her understanding of radical devotion to Christ and fueled her own commitment, years later, to spread the gospel. I'm grateful for this biography that retells a story of radical obedience, setting a standard for generations to come. May it inspire a new generation to trust and obey their Lord.

Valerie Elliot Shepard
Daughter of Jim and Elisabeth Elliot; author/speaker

This is a deeply moving biography, written from the family's perspective, of the young American missionaries John and Betty Stam and their death in China in 1934. It is an utterly tragic story, not least because they were so recently married and had so recently become parents. Providing a personal perspective through use of never-before published photographs and documents, Andrew Montonera tells of their training, exemplary courage, and committed faith.

Iain Torrance
Pro-Chancellor, University of Aberdeen; President Emeritus, Princeton Theological Seminary; Extra Chaplain in Ordinary to Queen Elizabeth II

The story of missionaries John and Betty Stam is that of missionary lore. Their life and brutal death, and the miraculous rescue of their baby girl, Helen, literally captured the hearts of people around the world in 1934. Their inspiring story must not be lost to future generations. *By Life or by Death* by Andrew Montonera will make sure that does not happen. The book is beautifully written, captivating, and inspiring. I read it in an afternoon. My prayer is many who read this book will be moved to GO to the nations, following in the footsteps of these two heroes of the faith.

DANIEL L. AKIN
President, Southeastern Baptist Theological Seminary, Wake Forest, North Carolina

An account read with many tears. My parents and both set of grandparents were missionaries in North China, where I also spent my first six years growing up. These were dangerous times. John and Betty Stam's witness to their faith is extraordinary and in many ways uplifting. I could not put this book down. Even after their short lives and martyred deaths, their influence reached thousands known and unknown. A truly inspiring journey.

PATRICIA LIDDELL RUSSELL
Eldest daughter of Eric and Florence Liddell

BY LIFE OR

The Life and Legacy of John and Betty Stam

ANDREW MONTONERA

Foreword by James Hudson Taylor IV

BY DEATH

MOODY PUBLISHERS
CHICAGO

Some historical documents quote from the King James Version.

Edited by Kevin Mungons
Interior design: Puckett Smartt
Cover design by Faceout Studio, Molly von Borstel
Cover image: John Stam and Betty Stam (author's collection)
Cover texture of printer marks copyright © 2024 by Ben__Stevens/Shutterstock (1381268000). All rights reserved.
Cover texture of old paper copyright © 2024 by oatawa/Shutterstock (1927355441). All rights reserved.
Author photo: Sarah Barlow

Library of Congress Cataloging-in-Publication Data

Names: Montonera, Andrew, author.
Title: By life or by death : the life and legacy of John and Betty Stam /
  Andrew Montonera ; foreword by James Hudson Taylor, IV.
Description: Chicago : Moody Publishers, [2024] | Includes bibliographical
  references and index. | Summary: "One of the most incredible missionary
  stories of the 20th century. Using family scrapbooks and unpublished
  sources, Montonera recounts the courage and martyrdom of the Stams when
  they were kidnapped by Chinese soldiers and the miraculous tale of how
  their baby survived. Read this captivating tale of kingdom-focused
  lives"-- Provided by publisher.
Identifiers: LCCN 2024019139 (print) | LCCN 2024019140 (ebook) | ISBN
  9780802432766 (paperback) | ISBN 9780802472502 (ebook)
Subjects: LCSH: Stam, John Cornelius, 1907-1934. | Stam, Elisabeth Alden
  Scott, 1906-1934. | Missionaries--China--Biography. |
  Kidnapping--China--History--20th century. | BISAC: RELIGION / Christian
  Ministry / Missions | BIOGRAPHY & AUTOBIOGRAPHY / Religious
Classification: LCC BV3705.S68 M56 2024 (print) | LCC BV3705.S68 (ebook)
  | DDC 266.0092/2 [B]--dc23/eng/20240531
LC record available at https://lccn.loc.gov/2024019139
LC ebook record available at https://lccn.loc.gov/2024019140

Originally delivered by fleets of horse-drawn wagons, the affordable paperbacks from D. L. Moody's publishing house resourced the church and served everyday people. Now, after more than 125 years of publishing and ministry, Moody Publishers' mission remains the same—even if our delivery systems have changed a bit. For more information on other books (and resources) created from a biblical perspective, go to www.moodypublishers.com or write to:

Moody Publishers
820 N. LaSalle Boulevard
Chicago, IL 60610

1 3 5 7 9 10 8 6 4 2

Printed in the United States of America

CONTENTS

"He is no fool who gives what he cannot keep to gain that which he cannot lose."

T hese familiar words were written in the journal of famed missionary Jim Elliot, who was martyred by the Auca Indians in Ecuador on January 8, 1956. We don't know how much Elliot, together with his four colleagues who were also martyred on that fateful January morning, was influenced by the testimony of John and Betty Stam. Yet two things certainly tied them together: all lived consecrated lives to see the fulfillment of the Great Commission of Jesus Christ (Matt. 28:18–20), and all paid the ultimate sacrifice for their obedience—giving up what they could not keep in order to gain that which they could not lose!

For John and Betty Stam, God's calling upon their lives came during their studies at Moody Bible Institute. Being one year apart at Moody, John and Betty went as far as to call off their relationship in order to allow each other to follow God's leading without the undue pressure of expectations. Yet it was partnership in marriage and ministry that the Lord had placed upon their lives. Their respective graduations from Moody were followed by application and acceptance by the China Inland Mission (CIM) for missionary service.

The CIM was started in 1865 by my great-great-grandfather, J. Hudson Taylor, with a vision to see the gospel proclaimed amongst the nearly 400 million Chinese in China, especially those in the inland provinces. Seeing eternity in the balance for each of these 400 million Chinese, Taylor prayed that the Lord would grant skillful and willing workers (1 Chron. 28:21) to the newly formed mission agency. He prayed their total dependence upon God's faithful provision, committed to the speediest evangelization of China's millions. Many years later, it was this same vision and passion for the evangelization of China's millions that caused John and Betty Stam, first separately, then together, to dedicate their lives to see Christ proclaimed in China.

Following language study, CIM leadership designated the Stams for missionary service in the province of Anhui (formerly romanized as Anhwei), where they served indefatigably in evangelism and church planting together for just over a year, followed by the ultimate sacrifice in the giving of their lives for the gospel. The story of their missionary service as well as evidential martyrdom at the hand of communist bandits has been well-told by Hudson Taylor's daughter-in-law, Geraldine Guinness Taylor, in *The Triumph of John and Betty Stam*, a book that has impacted countless others to consecrated lives and missionary service since its first printing in June 1935.

In 2006, I had the honor of traveling to the Anhui Province, to the very city where John and Betty Stam paid the price for their obedience to God's call upon their lives. There on a hill just outside the township of Miaoshou (formerly Miaosheo) stood the spot where, on that cold December morning in 1934, communist bandits brutally snuffed out the lives of these two young missionaries, orphaning an infant baby girl. As I stood in the very field where the Stams gave their lives, it was as if I was transported back to the days of Joshua, to when he was commanded by God to remove his shoes for he was standing on holy ground (Josh. 5). This place was hallowed by the shedding of the blood of these fearless servants of the risen Lord. Surely their lives and deaths call upon us to dedicate our lives afresh to His Great Commandment and His Great Commission.

Yet at the same time, as so aptly put by the church father Tertullian, "the blood of the martyrs is the seed of the church." In years prior, Betty's father passed on a poem entitled "Afraid? Of What?" to John. The final stanza of this poem, commemorating another missionary martyred in China, closes with these poignant words:

> *Afraid? Of what?*
> *To do by death what life could not—*
> *Baptize with blood a stony plot,*
> *Till souls shall blossom from the spot?*
> *Afraid? of that?*

If one was to return to Miaoshou and to the province of Anhui today, they would quickly find how many souls have blossomed from that spot. Both the growth of the church in Anhui and across China, as well as a growing burden for cross-cultural missions, is well-attested by many. John and Betty have surely not labored and died in vain. Rather, the fruit of their labors continue to this day.

It is this same powerful story that Andrew Montonera, a relative of John and Betty Stam, has now taken up, to tell with fresh eyes and a contemporary perspective. By divine providence, Andrew and I connected via social media in the fall of 2021. In subsequent communication, Andrew shared how he was first stirred by the story of John and Betty Stam, leading him to gather further information from archives housed at various Christian institutions as well as privately owned material from the Stam family. The result of Andrew's labor is the book you now hold. As each reader will quickly find, the triumph of John and Betty Stam, freshly told, will reveal again the truth of how a life committed to the gospel can ultimately change the world.

James Hudson Taylor IV
China Evangelical Seminary
Taoyuan, Taiwan

I can't remember when I first learned of my connection to John and Betty Stam—not exactly, at least. I do recall the visits as a young boy to my grandparents' home in the Chicago suburb of Mount Prospect, Illinois—with its memorable family gatherings, games in the backyard, and various work projects. Walking up to the second floor I could see a wall lined with family photos. I vividly recall a bookcase in my grandmother's office that contained a glass case with some of the frailest books I'd ever seen. I was just learning to read, but the aged bindings called out to me. In a house full of many old books, I could tell these were different.

"What are these books for?" I curiously asked one afternoon.

After a pause, my grandmother softly replied, "Those belonged to Grandpa Stam's brother who was killed in China."

Pulling a book out, she carefully opened the cover to reveal a signature, John C. Stam. Underneath was stamped a four-line message:

> John C. Stam
> Rescued from the Loot
> Tsingteh China
> Dec. 1934

My step-great-grandfather was Cornelius Stam, the closest sibling to John Stam in both age and relationship. Born in 1908, Cornelius became a pastor, author, and radio Bible teacher, best known for his views on dispensationalism. To be honest, I don't like using the word *step* when I explain all of this since I'm the closest thing he had to a biological great-grandson.

Cornelius was married to Henrietta Winter, who died in 1971. Six years later he married my mother's maternal grandmother, Ruth Wahlstrom, also widowed. Cornelius never had children with his first wife and as a result adopted our family as his own. We usually called him Neil, and as I was growing up, my mother and I affectionately referred to him as "Grandpa Stam," which he loved.

My family's direct association with Neil began through unique circumstances years prior when, in 1956, the Wahlstroms—consisting of Irving, Ruth, and their daughter, Grace—moved to Elmwood Park, Illinois. Two years later, Ruth began working part-time at the Berean Bible Society, a radio and publishing ministry, located only a couple blocks from the Wahlstrom home. Neil founded the Berean Bible Society in 1940 and subsequently moved the organization to Chicago in 1953 to reach a broader audience. The Wahlstroms had been good friends with another couple involved in the ministry, and on Christmas Day 1959, they were all invited to the Stam home for dinner.

That evening Neil gifted my grandmother two books that would not only be the introduction to her hosts' immediate family but also influence her for years to come. She could never have imagined that eighteen years later she'd be spending Christmas Day again with her mom now as Mrs. Stam and Neil as her stepfather.

In 1993, my great-grandparents settled into Windsor Park Manor, a retirement community in Carol Stream, Illinois. As the years went by their health started to decline, and by the time Neil died in 2003, he was the last Stam of his generation.

I grew up hearing the stories from an early age, but eventually came to understand how the truths behind this couple and their families so greatly affected my own. The martyrdom of John and Betty Stam is one of the most notable missionary tales of the twentieth century. Their unexpected deaths were both a shocking and life-altering despair for family and friends, yet the courage shown through the tribulation surrounding them inspired believers around the world. From December 1934 and the few years after, there was no bigger story in evangelicalism that carried such a large media presence and left an established mark on the global church. In a period where social reporting was always on the move, the world was not prepared for such a captivating account of Christian missionaries. It might seem hard to believe there was a point in time when you couldn't step inside an American church and not have the Stam name resonate with nearly everyone in the congregation.

Shortly after their deaths, Lewis Sperry Chafer, cofounder of Dallas Theological Seminary, wrote: "We have never had, so far as I know, a similar event which has called forth more public interest and comment than this has done."

Years later, it amazes me how the Stams continue to encourage people, and not only those in missions work. In a world full of uncertainty, many have been able to find hope in their example to live a life of unconventional faith.

Their story has been told as Christian lore for generations, but surprisingly, many basic details of this couple's impact have not been fully reexamined since first published in the 1930s. Like many stories, the details have become blurry with each retelling, leading to a good bit of misinformation over the years, and often with undocumented or conflicting sources. Hoping to recover the truth and discover new pieces of my spiritual heritage along the way, I started searching through my family's books, informal collections of memorabilia, and photo albums. After visiting collections at institutions and further researching those who were influenced, I understood the importance of a new biography that used as many original sources as possible to gain a new perspective. While I took inspiration from the books about John and Betty that came before, I felt there was so much potential in exploring for both historical and cultural context.

I also had help from several descendants of those associated with John and Betty to whom I'm grateful. Many of the events, personal writings, and photographs presented have never been published before. If the reader is already familiar with John and Betty Stam, this new material provides candid insight into their life and perspective on faith. On the other hand, perhaps you aren't familiar with these two missionaries. For those people I believe there's a reason you discovered this biography, wherever you're at. I've encountered many today, especially of more recent generations, who have never heard the names John and Betty Stam.

Their narrative is not only a challenge for believers to commit their whole selves to the gospel of Christ—it also shows the humanity behind their writing and poetic ability. Their brief lives on earth became a timeless story that endures in the hearts of children and some of the most respected theologians and preachers alike. Biographies give us a unique vantage point of what shaped these people. Whatever your age, relationship status, or occupation— you can gain practical knowledge from the discipline and suffering the Stams endured for their first true calling.

I can attest firsthand there are parts of John and Betty's life we'll never know, nor understand why certain events took place. Why did God use their love for the Chinese people the way He did? Why did the harsh reality of the martyrs' deaths reap the blessings of life upon others?

If you don't know their story, I'll forewarn that you might be left with lingering questions. I hope those passionate feelings of the unknown make your heart churn in a way that longs to understand God's will—like it did mine.

As I went through the Stams' books, letters, and possessions, an overwhelming presence of the Spirit reminded me of the faith I needed to surrender everything to the same Lord they served. By His grace, I experienced again the wonder, sorrow, and triumph that an innocent boy felt at his grandparents' place all those years ago.

How could these two ordinary individuals who had so much to live for— adored by friends, family, and peers alike—die so young and still be used to impact the world?

I pray a piece of that answer lies within the life and legacy of this consecrated couple. And as an extended descendant, I share in the joy that comes from a heart given for the sake of the gospel. I've attempted to tell their story with truthfulness, clarity, sympathy, and respect to all those involved. My deepest desire is that this preservation can be held by future generations, who as a result can benefit from the testimony of John and Betty Stam.

Andrew Montonera
Lake Zurich, Illinois

At Any Cost

John and Betty Stam, along with the six Chinese people who lived with them, had already eaten breakfast. John was planning to finish correspondence early that Thursday morning, while Betty was preparing a bath for their nearly three-month-old daughter with the help of the Stams' maid, Mei Tsong-fuh. The cook, Li Ming-chin, was busy at work in the kitchen. Li's wife, mother, and two children started their daily activities accordingly.

The Stams' missionary residence on the east side of Tsingteh (Jingde today), China, exhibited an all-familiar quiet scene. The day started out like any other. John and Betty were settled in Tsingteh for two weeks and looking forward to continuing their work with young children and church services in the southern part of the Anhwei Province (Anhui today).

Around eight that morning, a messenger from the town magistrate appeared at the Stam home to inform them that the Communist Red Army was about sixty miles away the previous night. At nine-thirty, the magistrate sent a second message telling them the Red Army was now within four miles of the city. John stepped outside their house and walked the street to see for himself, unsure about the conflicting reports. The Stam servants went out to get sedan chairs just to be prepared, in case they needed to use the wheelless vehicles for escape. Rumors had swirled for weeks regarding bandit activity, but John and Betty had been assured of their own safety.

Without any sign or speculative warning, the Red Army breached the city by eleven. A few of the soldiers climbed ladders to scale the city wall and quickly unlocked the east gate. Gunshots rang out as turmoil began in the streets. The district magistrate dressed himself as a farmer and retreated out the west gate, as most of the chair-bearers had also fled. John and Betty intended to exit the same gate, but there wasn't enough time. John and Li closed the doors within and barred them from anyone outside, then John and Betty knelt with their servants in prayer.

The courtyard that extended around the Stams' house was surrounded by four windowless brick walls. Soon, communist soldiers began to batter against the door at the back of the courtyard, breaking through after a half-dozen blows. As soon as the soldiers started banging on the Stams' door, John decided it was best to try and entertain them rather than have theirs kicked in. "Whether we entertain them or not, it's all over," Li said. John opened the door to greet them as four young soldiers immediately forced their way in. The soldiers were dressed in a mixture of gray and black uniforms. One soldier, an officer, was dressed better than the others, wearing a gray overcoat.

Introducing himself to the soldiers, John explained that he had just moved to town and was there to serve God. The conversation was civil at first, with the soldiers politely sharing their own names. The soldiers then inquired about any money the family might have, which John immediately turned over. Asking about anything else of value they might possess, John also surrendered favored items including a clock, watch, camera, and flashlight. He calmly proceeded to ask the soldiers if they were hungry. Betty came in from the kitchen to serve tea and cakes, but the courtesy was a useless gesture. Not having anything else to offer, John's hands were bound, and he was carried off to the magistrate's prison, which the Reds took over. Before John was taken away, he and Betty were able to stand and pray together in the small gathering around them. More soldiers then entered the home, tying together in bundles whatever seemed of value or use for their cause. Shortly after, the soldiers returned for Betty and the infant.

The maid and cook pleaded to go with the Stams but were deterred at the threat of being shot. Pointing their guns at the maid and cook, the soldiers asked why a Chinese person would be concerned about a foreigner. "It is better that you stay here," Betty whispered to their maid and cook. "If any trouble comes to us, look after the baby." That afternoon around four, John was allowed to return home, again under the supervision of four soldiers, to retrieve food and additional clothing for their child. The maid commented that many of their possessions had been stolen. "It doesn't matter," John affirmed. "God is high above all in heaven. Our Father knows. These things don't matter a bit. Don't be afraid, Mrs. Mei. You sleep with old Mrs. Li tonight."

Later, back at the magistrate's prison, John wrote a letter to officials at China Inland Mission in Shanghai, notifying them they had been captured and were being held for ransom:

Tsingteh, Anhwei
December 6, 1934

```
China Inland Mission,
Shanghai

Dear Brethren,

My wife, baby, and myself are today in the hands of the
Communists, in the city of Tsingteh. Their demand is
twenty thousand dollars for our release.

All our possessions and stores are in their hands, but
we praise God for peace in our hearts and a meal tonight.
God grant you wisdom in what you do, and us fortitude,
courage, and peace of heart. He is able, and a wonderful
Friend in such a time.

Things happened so quickly this A.M. They were in the city
just a few hours after the ever-persistent rumors really
became alarming, so that we could not prepare to leave in
time. We were just too late.

The Lord bless and guide you, and as for us, may God be
glorified whether by life or by death.
```

In Him,
John C. Stam

CHAPTER ONE

A Heritage from Holland

John Stam's spiritual heritage began at an early age through the devotion of his parents' commitment to raising up a God-fearing family. Their desire for others to know the gospel message allowed them to have an impact on all their children, each one eventually serving in Christian ministry.

John's father, Peter Stam, was born in Holland on May 23, 1866. He grew up in the village of 't Zand, North Holland, Netherlands, and worked the family-owned tavern run by his father. Being in the family for three generations at this point, the tavern included its own theatre, store, and cafe. Because his father needed entertainers, Peter was naturally brought up in show business. For a period, he traveled throughout Holland, Belgium, and Luxembourg—making people laugh, but all too often with a heavy heart. At the time, North Holland had little to no gospel literature. Peter noticed the people close to him partook in activities that only brought temporary satisfaction, including those who attended the local once-a-month church services. Peter later testified to his children that he never once heard the gospel preached in North Holland. In reality, the local state church couldn't decide or agree on what to teach. They often alternated between a Protestant minister, Catholic priest, and a Jewish rabbi. The topics preached ranged from politics to various books, and after the service the preacher would go to the Stam tavern to drink and shoot pool with the others. Peter wanted a change from the life he had always known. Like many European immigrants at the time, he came to America to start anew with the chance of fortune and stability.

On March 29, 1890, Peter Stam sailed first class from Holland to America aboard the *SS Spaarndam*. He was twenty-three years old and had 900 Dutch

19

guilders in his pocket. Originally planning to settle in Long Island, New York, Peter decided to board with a Dutch family he was in contact with in Paterson, New Jersey. He was grateful for the family's hospitality, except for one thing. They read the Bible at every evening meal and chose passages for him to read aloud. Frustrated, he eventually left the boarding house complaining that he didn't pay board money to hear that book read. To get away from the Bible and learn English faster, Peter boarded with an English-speaking family in Hackensack, New Jersey, and began to learn to read and speak English at a quicker pace. Little did Peter know what was in store for him.

While reading a magazine on a park bench the morning of July 4, 1890, Peter met a zealous woman named Margaret Neighmond, who was sitting on the other end of the bench. She happened to be a neighbor of the family Peter boarded with. Unable to understand a certain word from the magazine, Peter asked Margaret for help. Discovering he was a Hollander trying to learn English, she commented that she had a book for him. She explained, "It has two columns on each page. The left column is in Dutch; you can understand that. Then you go to the opposite column, and you'll find the same thing printed in English. It's published especially for immigrants like you. I'll be glad to give it to you if you'd like." Peter was elated, and eagerly took the book home with him.

Not long after, he realized that this was the same book he had come to loathe. Peter would often tell his children how close he came to throwing the book in the garbage. Determined by any means to learn English, however, Peter continued reading the Dutch-English New Testament. He eventually came to love the book so much, rejoicing not only in the knowledge gained but also the assurance of salvation. Peter reflected on that time:

> The book told me that I was a sinner. Of course, my proud nature rebelled. It told me I was lost. I tried not to believe it; but as I read on, I had to be honest with myself, and confess that I was indeed a sinner. My life had been lived entirely to self . . .
>
> But the Book told me that God loved me; that He "so loved the world (and that meant me) that he gave his only begotten Son, that whoever believeth

in him should not perish (that too meant me) but have everlasting life."
(John 3:16)

Then and there I closed with the offer. I believed the Word of God and
received Christ as my own personal Savior. I surrendered my life to Him
who died for me, and began by His grace to live for others, because the love
of Christ constrained me.

Peter shifted through various jobs during those first couple years in
America. Carpentry appealed to him, but he also worked in sales. One day
when selling jewelry at homes in Paterson, he was told by an older Christian
woman living on the second floor to come upstairs. Ascending the flight of
stairs, Peter sold a watch to the woman for her daughter, who he quickly got
to know as Amelia Williams.

Amelia Elisabeth Alletta Williams immigrated with her immediate
family from Rotterdam, Holland, in October 1888. They were part French
Huguenot by descent. Amelia's father had died from smallpox a decade and
a half prior to them immigrating, and her mother supported the family by
providing nursing services to wealthy families in the Paterson area. A friendship spontaneously developed between Peter and Amelia, and the two were
married on January 7, 1892, at the home of Rev. Peter Van Vlaanderen of
First Christian Reformed Church of Paterson.

One Saturday evening shortly after their first child, Peter Jr., was born,
Mr. Stam was building a cradle that would serve all his children. Unexpectedly
he got a visit from his carpentry employer. Peter received word from his boss
that he had to present himself at work the following morning to finish a rush
job. A difficult decision was presented, but Mr. Stam gracefully explained that
he could not come in on Sunday, since he was a Christian, and the Lord's Day
must be observed. He told his boss that he'd work until midnight that night
and begin at midnight the next but would not provide labor on Sundays.
"Then you are out of work," was the angry retort. Mr. Stam accepted this and
acknowledged that his faith in the Lord would supply his needs.

Shortly before Peter fell asleep that night, a messenger from a former
employer knocked at the front door and asked if he'd come back to work for

him—at a higher wage than before, and right away on Monday morning. Peter never forgot this experience and continually used it as a reminder for his children to trust in the Lord, not counting the cost. In May 1893, Peter's father came from Holland to see his son and his new family. Before his father returned home, he gave his son finances to help purchase land to build houses on. Through his carpentry experience and the money borrowed at interest from his father, Peter continued to gain work and became a successful builder. The flourishing business developed to include a lumberyard and insurance office. This was a great blessing to the family.

Peter and Amelia lived in two different homes their first fourteen years of marriage. The second of these homes stood at 13 N. 8th St. in Hawthorn, New Jersey. This soon became known as the corner of 8th St. and Stam's Alley, due to Peter's thriving lumber business, where he would build over a hundred homes in the area. On January 25, 1906, the growing family moved into a new fourteen-room house Peter built in the Temple Hill section of Paterson. The house at 146 N. 7th St. was the tallest in Temple Hill, reached by a flight of steps leading from the street. This home is where John Stam grew up and developed his faith.

CHAPTER TWO

Humble Beginnings

Peter and Amelia Stam eventually had nine children—six sons and three daughters. Their second daughter, Catherine, died of bronchial pneumonia at ten months old. As parents they intended to teach their children the Word of God and conservative values from an early age. The family motto was Ebenezer—"Hitherto hath the Lord helped us" (1 Sam. 7:12). Peter created and installed a stained-glass window with the phrase in the Stam house on N. 7th St. as a reminder for his family to be faithful with all that God has given. Not far from their home was the Christian grammar school where all the children were enrolled.

At home a Bible was placed on the table for each person during their meals, three times a day. Before the food was served, a prayer was given, and a chapter read by each family member. The Bible was the foundation of the Stam household. Books and music were the other pieces that bound the family together. "We certainly were brought up on books," recalled the eldest sister, Clazina, "and we all had to take music lessons. Father spared no expense to give us the best in these ways. And how we did enjoy our family orchestra!" The siblings would go on to use their musical abilities in various facets of ministry while growing up and into adulthood.

To safeguard their hearts from potentially negative spiritual influences, Mr. and Mrs. Stam chose not to have a radio in their home and discouraged their children from smoking, dancing, and attending movies. To try and make up for their children "missing out" on these worldly activities, the family often took sailing trips along the East Coast and went sightseeing in New York City. Peter and Amelia wanted their children to know how much they were appreciated, but that their work for Christ was the end reward that should fulfill their desire to serve Him.

During this time, Peter was active in Paterson's Third Christian Reformed Church as an elder and Sunday school teacher. Even as his business endeavors were taking off, Peter wanted to start his own ministry to help the underprivileged Paterson community. His ministry started as an outreach to Jews by distributing Christian literature and evangelizing through his personal testimony. Peter established the Star of Hope Mission in 1913, which served his ultimate vision of bringing the gospel to the residents around Paterson. The name Star of Hope was suggested by Rev. Van Vlaanderen after conversing with Peter about the ministry. A neatly furnished mission hall was soon acquired where witnessing could be done to those coming in from the street. As work for the mission grew, Peter recruited volunteers from local churches who helped reach the homeless, local prisons, hospitals, and various charity groups. The family always respected Mr. Stam's authority, never questioning it. Attending the Star of Hope meetings was expected of the children, even if their father didn't say so. Peter later started three missions in the Netherlands to help teach and equip others.

John Cornelius Stam, born January 18, 1907, was the Stams' seventh child and fifth son. As part of the Christian Reformed Church tradition, John was dedicated to the Lord when he was baptized at less than a month old. He grew up attending the same grammar school as his siblings where Scripture and Christian principles were reinforced. As a student, John was a quiet yet courteous boy who was sharp when it came to fine details, and always eager to help those in need. At a young age he would sew a button on his own clothing rather than going to his mother to do it, or take the initiative of uprooting a tree himself without being asked. After John graduated from the grammar school, his father offered to help him financially to seek out higher education. John wanted to pursue business instead and attended the Drake Business School for two years, where he gained experience in bookkeeping and stenography. Though only fifteen years old when enrolled, he was already over six feet tall and possessed the look of a young man in his early twenties. Growing up in this Christian environment, John was expected to adopt the lifestyle of his older siblings—but this wasn't the case, as he struggled with inner doubts about his work ability. He didn't get involved as much as his siblings at the mission his father started, and he questioned whether he'd be able to make it in the business world.

As the spiritual need for the city grew, John's father wanted to build a mission hall that could hold more people and be an even greater outreach to the community. Peter acquired a piece of land with an old livery stable and planned to renovate it for his mission purposes. With a growing number of Christian supporters and much of his own finances, the building was bought for $12,000. On April 21, 1919, the new Star of Hope Mission opened on 34 Broadway in Paterson. At the same time, Peter disposed of his lumber and contracting business—and because the Lord had prospered his previous work, he labored without salary.

Peter took the family motto of Ebenezer—"Hitherto hath the Lord helped us"—and revised it to "Hitherto hath the Lord done it all." The new building had a total of nineteen rooms used for offices, Sunday school, sewing classes, and other needs. The most impressive addition was the auditorium, large enough to seat six hundred people, where many evangelistic meetings were conducted in the decades to follow. The Stam residence often hosted the many guest speakers who appeared at the Star of Hope, including such notable names as Geraldine Taylor, Thomas Lambie, Donald Barnhouse, Arno C. Gaebelein, and Harry A. Ironside. Meeting these missionaries and Bible teachers left an indelible impression on many of the children growing up in their teens and twenties.

Thomas Houston, a blind evangelist from Scotland, gave a series of sermons at the mission during the spring of 1922. Seated in the last row, John, Neil, and their older brother Jacob (Jake) Stam listened intently one Sunday evening. John and Neil were so convicted by the preaching that before the meeting finished they decided to slip out during the last hymn, afraid Pastor Houston might give an altar call to receive Christ. They went home without saying a word to each other, leaving the rest of their family at the revival.

Later that night a woman called the Stam home with some troubling news: "Mr. Stam, I'm so sorry to have to tell you this, but I'm afraid John and Neil have been drinking. I saw them come home and they were both staggering." John and Neil were under so much conviction of sin that the brothers had unsteady feet on their walk home. Peter was relieved after his sons explained the situation. Jacob prayed with his younger brothers to receive the gift of salvation, and afterward wrote in his study Bible opposite Acts 16:31: "'And thy house'—May 28, 1922, Cornelius Stam and John Stam decided for Christ, believing on Him." The rest of the family shared in the joy that night with John and Neil.

After receiving this gift, John knew that it had to be shared. The calling didn't start out easy for him though. The next day John went to the business school, and while at his desk he pondered the sins and struggle of self-righteousness he dealt with as a teenager. John had witnessed drunkards and people ignorant of the gospel getting saved through his family's ministry, but up to that point had thought of himself as morally superior. In years prior, John and his younger brother would avoid many of the city streets where their father and Christian friends were holding open-air meetings, embarrassed they might be seen by classmates. Soon after his conversion, John was surprised that he hadn't seen any of the meetings being held like he was used to. Inwardly curious, he asked his father why the band was not out preaching. "It's up to you, John, to make a beginning," was Mr. Stam's response. With this realization, John knew he had to take a stand for what he believed. Nearly all the summer evenings which followed, John and Neil were seen fearlessly preaching together on the various street corners of Paterson, for a great burden had been lifted off their hearts.

John completed his training at the business college the following year. Over the course of the next six years he worked as a stenographer and clerk in several Paterson and New York business homes, while also volunteering at the Star of Hope Mission. In New York his office windows overlooked Battery Park, where he saw the shipping yards with their heavy freight being transported around the world. Sometimes he'd walk down the city's notable boulevards such as Broadway and Fifth Avenue, always expanding his worldview. He once walked the entire length of Manhattan Island. Though his family was never much for worldly entertainment, John's parents always supported music, so they encouraged their children to attend concerts. In their late teens, John and Neil would often take the train on Saturday afternoons to attend concerts at Carnegie Hall. One such performance John attended featured Sergei Rachmaninoff, who played his famous composition, "Prelude in C-sharp Minor," bringing seven encores.

New York City established its place in the Roaring Twenties, and John witnessed much of the consumerism of that era. Realizing the world had so many lost people and wanting to devote himself to full-time ministry, John announced his resignation in spring 1929. The office employer pleaded with him to stay, not wanting to lose a dedicated and reliable worker, but John's mind was made up.

Shortly after his resignation, Peter and Amelia Stam made a trip to Holland, leaving John and Neil to oversee the Star of Hope Mission. Not long after his parents left, however, John realized the challenge of running the ministry. One morning as John prayed about the matter, he stated, "I am the wrong man to have anything to do with this." Just then he lifted his eyes and noticed a plaque hanging on the opposite wall. The plaque had been on the wall for months, but John never took notice of its message. The text was Psalm 18:32: "It is God that girdeth me with strength, and maketh my way perfect." The verse reminded John to faithfully carry on the task assigned to him for the family mission, but he also realized in that moment how much he had to learn about vocational ministry. At age twenty-two, most would have believed John was content with life, with financial stability and his family close by, but the desire for further biblical training was heavily put upon his heart. After praying a few more weeks while volunteering time to the Star of Hope that summer, John enrolled at Moody Bible Institute in Chicago.

John Stam's Testimony

September 3, 1932

I thank God tonight that I am a Christian. I don't know how many times in the last weeks and months that thought has come to my mind and heart. But no matter how much it comes it ought to be there a great deal more. I thank God I am a Christian and I thank Him for a Christian home; for father and mother who brought me up in the ways of the Lord. I look back at the time when I was in deep conviction of sin in May 1922; when week after week I had been hearing the Word of God. A blind man was here preaching the Word of God. How many times I sat in that corner and wanted to come forward, but I didn't. One morning after he had given the invitation I was sitting in the back with Jake. He asked the unsaved to stand and then he asked Christians to stand up. I never did like that way of doing things and I don't now. But I didn't have the courage of my convictions to stay seated and I stood up and Jake turned around and said, "Praise the Lord; you're a Christian. Why don't you go up?" But I didn't want to do that. I let it go through that I had taken the Lord Jesus. How happy everyone was at home! But I wasn't really saved until the next day at business school. I realized I was a hypocrite and did not have the courage of my convictions, and let my people believe I had accepted Christ when I hadn't. How I thank Him for the message of salvation and that He saved even me.

Just these last three or four weeks I had the privilege of living among unsaved people day and night. I have worked with unsaved people, but never lived with them. I got to see something of the beauty of our salvation. Oh to know God has given us something real! As I looked into their lives and talked with them and heard their hopes and aims, having nothing in life that was worthwhile; and if they were going out through the shadows they had nothing and as I talked with the moralist, the fine men who went to church, the greatest thing he thought a man could to show people he was a Christian was to give a big check to his employees. I came out of that with another thing to thank the Lord Jesus for; not only that I am saved, but that I have a message to bring to people that have nothing real in life; who have a certain amount of fear because when they came close up to the end they had fear, and if believed would bring them into the glory of an eternal salvation. How I thank God for that wonderful salvation that is in the Lord Jesus Christ.

In 1929 Dad went to Holland with mother, to see the missions and on a little vacation trip. He left the mission in charge of my brother Neil and myself. After dad had been out to sea about a day or two, I began to realize that I was not the right kind of a person to have anything to do with the mission. I was up in that room having prayer, and I was beginning to see, as we will see, trouble among the workers and meetings dwindling in interest and helpfulness, and I was saying, "I am the wrong man to have anything to do with this." Suddenly I lifted up my eyes and there was a text on the opposite wall. The text had been there for weeks and months but never had I noticed it before. This was the verse:

Psalm 18:32. It is God that girdeth me with strength, and maketh my way perfect.

Oh what a blessing that verse was to me that morning! To realize it wasn't in my strength, but it was God. God was the one who did it. David wrote that, and David was the man who slew a lion and bear. It was that man who said it was God that girded him with that strength. When we get to realize we have no might, to them will He give power; to the one that is faint, to that one He will give strength.

Several weeks ago when I came home, I went to my room and was rather sick and tired and not much fit to go into the work of the Lord, not even in China. I opened the draw in the desk and the very first text that met my eyes was the one that I saw up in that room. And this time I needed it more than before. Oh men and women, I want to ask you to do this: that God will ever keep me where His power can flow through. I know how it is to become so busy with things that we are unable and do not find time to dig into His Word and to spend time in prayer with Him. But if I don't do that, what is the use of going out at all? What is the use if God doesn't gird me with strength? Will you not pray that every day I may find that fresh strength that comes from Him. That I shall feel the need of Himself each day and have to go aside and spend time alone with Him. Aren't you, aren't we all glad that tonight we can say, "It is God that girdeth us with strength!"

Pray for me. Thank you.

John C. Stam

CHAPTER THREE

Growing Up Overseas

Much like her husband, John, Betty Stam was raised in a Christian environment. Betty's father, Charles Ernest Scott, was born June 22, 1876, in Albion, Michigan. The son of a Civil War officer, Charles grew up in a Presbyterian home where he developed an early commitment to memorizing Scripture and an interest in world history. After graduating from Alma College, he went on to earn a master of arts degree in history from the University of Pennsylvania in 1899. He then became a fellow at the University of Munich in Germany for a year, where he met a young American woman named Clara Emily Heywood. Returning to the States, Charles attended Princeton Theological Seminary and studied under distinguished theologian Benjamin B. Warfield. After hearing countless sermons about China from professors and visiting missionaries, Charles gained a desire to reach that land with the gospel.

Graduating from Princeton with a doctor of philosophy degree in 1903, he married Clara Heywood on September 9 at a church in his bride's hometown of Holyoke, Massachusetts. Despite being presented with prominent academic opportunities, Charles felt called to devote his life to missionary service after being ordained. He first served as a Presbyterian home missionary in the woods of Michigan and later as pastor of the First Church of Albion for two years.

Charles and Clara's first child, Elisabeth (Betty) Alden Scott, was born on February 22, 1906, in Albion. Her middle name was given in memory of John and Priscilla Alden, direct ancestors of Clara's and early settlers to America on the *Mayflower*. In addition to generations of family heritage on the East Coast, Clara also grew up in a strong Christian home. When

Betty was just six months old, her parents served as missionaries under the Presbyterian Board USA, carrying out evangelistic work and Bible teaching.

Charles and Clara didn't believe it was best to serve as missionaries within the confines of foreign culture, so they brought their best American possessions to China—including books, paintings, numerous wedding gifts, and their piano. They arrived safely on October 4, 1906, but their household items—coming on another ship—were lost when the vessel sank during a typhoon. Taking the loss hard, the couple realized that God was weaning them from material things. They first lived in the city of Tsingtao (Qingdao today), located along the coast in the northern province of Shandong. Four more children were born in China; two daughters, Helen and Beatrice (Bunny), and two sons, Francis (Laddie) and Kenneth (Ken).

Betty Scott possessed a unique way with words and began writing poetry as a young girl. One example of her early talent is "The Lilac," a short poem about beauty and nature written at eight years old:

The Lilac

Pretty little flower,
  Blossoming in the spring,
With your leaves and dainty flowers,
  You're a pretty thing.

When the winter's here you go,
  But come again in spring,
Then you see the children dear,
  And hear the bluebirds sing.

Dr. and Mrs. Scott, though heavily involved in ministry duties, invested a great deal of time to the upbringing of their five children. The family motto was "Do it together," which is precisely how they approached life. There were hardly any other children within three miles of them, so they quickly developed a strong family bond. After breakfast each morning they had family prayers, in which each child would take turns praying and choosing the songs to sing. At eleven each day, Charles took a break from his ministry tasks and played with his children. After a midday dinner, Charles and Clara would both read illustrated children's books to them. Each child was required to lie down for an hour as their imaginations carried them off into a story.

Betty's youngest sister, Helen, told of that time: "I think that our father and mother must have taken their career as parents more seriously than most people; for as we look back upon it all—the careful training, the many activities they shared with us, and the mental attitudes they so carefully instilled— we marvel at the work they must have put into it."

As a young adult, Betty wrote "To Father and Mother," a poem expressing her love and appreciation for her upbringing during this period.

To Father and Mother

My words, dear Father, precious Mother,
*   May God select from His rich store.*
I am, because you loved each other—
*   Oh, may my love unite you more!*

When I was born, brimmed the bright water,
*   For pain and joy, in eyes gray-blue.*
(A tiny bud of you, a daughter;
*   And yet, distinct, a person too!)*

In pain and joy and love upwelling,
*   You treasured me against your heart;*
And I, bewildered beyond telling,
*   Grew calm and slept, with tears astart.*

As life grew bigger, I stood firmer,
*   With legs apart, eyes round and wide.*
You told me all I asked, a learner
*   Who was not ever satisfied!*

Throughout my childhood flitted fairies
*   Of sunshine and the open air,*
Came chubby sisters, cheeked with cherries,
*   And baby boys with kewpie-hair.*

We grew like colts and April saplings—
  Seeking rebelliously for Truth.
You loved and learned and stood beside us,
  And understood the shocks of youth.

As life grew mystical and magic
  And I walked dreamily on earth,
Ere I should wake to see the tragic,
  You planted, deep, ideals of worth.

You fed my mind, a flamelet tiny
  Yet keen and hungry, in a wood;
It seized and glowed and spread and crackled—
  And all the fuel in reach was good.

Somewhere beneath the loam of senses,
  A seed of Art you hoped was there,
Received the sun and rain and blossomed,
  All through your stimulating care.

But not content with mental culture,
  Seeing my spirit mourn in night,
You taught the Word and Way for sinners,
  Until Christ's Spirit brought me light.

Your loving courage never faltered,
  Your plans were gently laid aside,
That time my whole life-pattern altered
  Obedient to our Lord and Guide.

Your life for others, in each other,
  Shines through the world, pain-tarnished here;
As faithful stewards, Father, Mother,
  Your crown shall be unstained by tear.

Imagine, in God's certain Heaven,
  Your children, made forever glad,
Praising the Lord for having given
  The dearest parents ever had.

Those happy childhood years in Tsingtao eventually came to an end. As a teen, Betty attended the coeducational school in the Tungchow district (Tongzhou today) near Peking (Beijing today). Shortly after, the rest of the family moved to Tsinan (Jinan today) in 1918, and in time, Betty's siblings followed her to the school in Tungchow. The Scott children spent Christmas and most summers at their family's home in Tsinan. The rest of the time the family stayed at their seaside cottage in Peitaiho (Beidaihe today), where they spent their days swimming, playing tennis, reading, and assisting their father in secretarial work. During this period, Charles Scott wrote multiple books about his cultural experiences in China and the work to advance the gospel. One of his influential supporters was Woodrow Wilson, a past president of Princeton University and admired instructor, who became president of the United States in 1913. Wilson greatly respected Charles and asked for his advice about Western diplomacy with China. Between 1909 and 1919, Scott and Wilson corresponded at least a dozen and a half times.

When Betty was seventeen, her parents were due to take a furlough in the United States. The Scotts knew Betty was to finish high school and attend college in the States, so it might be the last year for a while they would get to spend together as a family. Desiring their children to experience other parts of the world, the family invested six full months between February and August in 1923 to travel across several countries in the Middle East and Europe, bound for America. The Scotts traveled from China through Hong Kong to visit Singapore, British Ceylon, Egypt, Palestine, Greece, Italy, Switzerland, France, and England.

They packed numerous experiences into those riveting months. They visited the tombs of the ancient pharaohs and rode donkeys across the plains of Egypt. They were amazed at the sight of a pageant in Venice to honor Benito Mussolini, the fascist dictator rising to power in Italy. Another major highlight was seeing Pope Pius XI in person at St. Peter's Basilica. During this period, Betty met a young Irishman who left a special impression on her. He had left his family to become an African missionary, and she was greatly attracted to his overflowing, Christ-filled spirit. The two of them corresponded for a while but eventually lost contact.

Some of Betty's memories from these experiences, as well as her sensible outlook on life, were put to words in her poem "Traveller's Song":

Traveller's Song

I sought for beauty o'er the earth,
  And found it everywhere I turned:
A precious stone from Singapore
  That sapphire shone and sapphire burned;
A Rajah's ransom it was worth.

Eternal grandeur brooded deep
  In Egypt's pyramids of stone,
And still I smell the orange bloom;
  I see the frosty stars that shone
And cooled the tranquil Nile to sleep.

I loved the skies of Italy,
  The swarthy, singing boatmen there,
The Virgins of the Renaissance,
  With grave, sweet eyes and golden hair –
The land of Art and Melody!

Lingers long into the night
  On snowy peaks the Alpine glow,
And every lake is loveliest,
  And there, amid the endless snow,
I picked the edelweiss so white.

Before a Chinese city gate,
  The entrance to an ancient town,
I saw the men fly dragon-kites;
  While, by the willows weeping down,
Their wives beat clothes, from dawn till late.

Then home I came, as though on wings,
  The joy of life in heart and eyes;
For, everything was glorified –
  The earth, the ocean, and the skies,
And even all the common things!

Charles and Clara Scott's successful emphasis on Christian ministry can also be seen in their children's global missionary work. Each one eventually served as missionaries in China. Writing about her time returning from the family's furlough, Helen Scott said, "All five of us children expected at that time to return to China as missionaries. Our parents never urged it, but it seemed the natural and right thing to do." While at the Chinese boarding school, Betty and Helen had studied Chinese for two years, learning to both read and write the language.

After arriving back to America, the Scotts resided in Springfield, Massachusetts, where Betty concluded her senior year of high school. For four months in the spring of 1924, Betty became seriously sick with inflammatory rheumatism, an autoimmune disease, causing inflammation around the joints, tendons, and bones. The illness left her heart so weakened that she was forced to lie flat on her back to ease the pain. It was during this time spent recovering at the home of family friends in Holyoke when she first realized her true love for poetry. Betty started actively writing more verses about her vast trips and life experiences.

CHAPTER FOUR

A Life Further Surrendered

B y September 1924, nearly a full year after the Scotts arrived in America on furlough, Betty's health had sufficiently recovered to allow her to enter Wilson College in Chambersburg, Pennsylvania. Established as a women's college in 1869 by Presbyterian pastors Tryon Edwards and James W. Wightman, the school came to be named after Sarah Wilson, a nearby resident of St. Thomas Township who provided two generous donations for the institution.

Betty's outstanding literary gifts and mature outlook on the world were warmly welcomed on campus, as she quickly gained the respect of her peers. During her years of study, Betty participated in many extracurriculars, becoming president of the college's literary society and associate editor of the society's publication. She served on the student government cabinet and was an active member of the Student Union. Bible classes were also required each year, allowing Betty to gain a better understanding of the Word she grew to know as a child.

In the month of July, between her first two years at Wilson, she attended a student conference at America's Keswick in New Jersey. It left a profound impact on her spiritual life, and she fully consecrated herself to the Lord. Betty listened to a variety of speakers, read books, and witnessed how others used their gifts to share the gospel. Afterward she wrote her parents about the experience:

> "Keswick" is over, but I trust never the message! Thank the Lord! I have now surrendered myself to the Lord more than I have ever realized was possible. Already He has wonderfully answered my prayers, in little things and in big ones. Nearly all the most unlikely boys and girls were won to consecrate

their lives to Him. The "Say-So Meeting" yesterday was simply triumphant. I have never realized that such victory was possible. The Way is just Christ— and complete consecration to His will in our lives. Among other things, I have dedicated to Him whatever I have of poetic or literary gift. Maybe He can use me along that line. Wouldn't it be wonderful! I have been greatly impressed by the way in which Mr. Harkness had dedicated his musical talents to the Lord.

Giving my life to Jesus makes me see what I ought to have done long ago, and I wonder how I can have been so dumb before. Now that sounds as though I were a perfect little angel, flapping my wings 'round! But, of course, I'm awfully imperfect still, or as one might put it, future-perfect—which means that there is promise for the future. Even now, when I put first the pleasure, interests and point of view of others, everything goes along most gaily. "Keswick" has been a wonderful revelation to me of how victorious the victorious life really is. Since being there I have had my prayers answered in most definite ways. Now the Lord is showing me how necessary it is to rise early in the morning to read His Word, and He is helping me to wake and get up in time to do so.

I don't know what God has in store for me. I really am willing to be an old-maid missionary, or an old-maid anything else, all my life, if God wants me to. It's as clear as daylight to me that the only worth-while life is one of unconditional surrender to God's will, and of living in His way, trusting His love and guidance.

At the Keswick conference, Betty adopted Philippians 1:21 as her life verse: "For me to live is Christ, and to die is gain." She also began praying that if it were God's will, nothing might prevent her from returning to China as a missionary. As a sophomore, she expounded on this subject, writing, "When we consecrate ourselves to God, we think we are making a great sacrifice, and doing lots for Him, when really we are only letting go some little, bitsie trinkets we have been grabbing, and when our hands are empty, He fills them full of His treasures."

Betty spent the summer of 1926 visiting friends in California while becoming further devoted in her faith. In October of that same year, she wrote a letter to her sister Beatrice expressing complete surrender to become a missionary. Even with all her activities and commitments, Betty excelled academically, graduating *magna cum laude* in 1928. Her sisters, Helen and Beatrice, graduated from Wilson in 1930 and 1933. Underneath Betty's senior yearbook photo was this witty caption:

> *A spirit of calm serenity,*
>   *A faith untroubled as faith can be,*
> *Creator of beautiful poetry,*
>   *Images we can feel and see,*
> *Cherry blossoms and Chinamen—*
> *'28's genius of the pen!*

Dr. Warren Nevius, professor of ethics and English Bible, recalled of her presence during those four years: "Perhaps what most alumnae will remember, aside from the gentleness of her demeanor, the fragrance of her loving spirit and the grace of her literary expression, will be the serenity and faith with which she lived among us; a serenity born of the deep peace of her own soul, and a faith that was founded upon a Rock. Values like this cannot perish."

Betty entered Moody Bible Institute in Chicago after her graduation from Wilson, desiring to gain further practical experience in witnessing for Christ. One of her sisters described her time there:

> She chose Moody's because she wanted to learn how to win souls to Christ, instead of just talking about it theoretically, or discussing the Bible in an abstract way. The course at Moody's gave her great spiritual poise, and the prison and street meetings, which her sensitive spirit dreaded, turned out to be a help and brought her no little joy.

Betty's friends from both Wilson and Moody remembered her as a sincere and formative individual. Students often sought her out as a confidant, appreciating her way of sharing opinions only after serious thought and prayer. Her dress, while always appropriate, was never flashy. She didn't wear jewelry or flowers in her hair, which was often parted to one side and tied together in a knot at the back of her neck.

While Betty maintained several friends and peers who admired her, she did have struggles during those years studying in the States. Like many missionary children, she was alone, removed from her parents. They weren't around to help her navigate many of the difficult life questions and circumstances she now faced as a young adult, and this caused her to rely on God alone. Betty's frequent outward calmness toward others didn't reflect the inner searching of her heart when beginning at Moody. In her first year, the needs of Africa, especially lepers, were pressed upon her heart. As much as she loved China, she feared that it was partly due to love of parents and home that influenced those feelings. Praying about the matter, Betty decided to listen to God's call and follow whatever doors He might open for her to serve. She was able to articulate this with a sense of further reassurance in her poem titled "My Testimony":

My Testimony

And shall I fear
  That there is anything that men hold dear
Thou would'st deprive me of,
  And nothing give in place?
That is not so—
  For I can see Thy face
And hear Thee now:

My child, I died for thee.
  And if the gift of love and life
You took from Me,
  Shall I one gracious thing withhold to all eternity
One beautiful and bright
  One pure and precious thing withhold?
My child, it cannot be.

Charles Scott's closest friends during most of his adult life were Philip E. Howard, Howard's brother in-law Charles G. Trumbull, and Howard's son Philip E. Howard Jr. All three were editors at *The Sunday School Times*, a Philadelphia-based Christian newspaper that was well-recognized by Protestants of the era. A few of Betty's poems during her years at Wilson and Moody, as well as her father's writings, were published in the popular weekly journal. American author and diplomat Henry Van Dyke Jr., who knew Charles Scott and frequently read the paper, was impressed with Betty's work. "These are real poems. If you will publish them, I will write the introduction," he penned to Dr. Scott. Years later, her parents reflected on their daughter's gifted ability, saying, "Betty was by nature shy and reticent, so would never have thought of offering her poems for publication. She delighted in jotting them down as the mood possessed her. In one of her letters home she expressed her desire to use to the glory of God whatever gifts He had given her."

Her first year at Moody, Betty wrote the autobiographical poem "Stand Still and See." After sending it to her father a year later she explained, "This poem expresses the distress of soul and fear of mind that were mine before I surrendered my all—even inmost motives, so far as I know—to God's control. The fourth stanza is His gracious acceptance of my unworthy self; the last tells of the joy, satisfaction, and peace of assured guidance that Christ my Savior gives me, now that He is Lord of my life."

Stand Still and See

> *I'm standing, Lord:*
> *There is a mist that blinds my sight*
> *Steep, jagged rocks, front, left and right,*
> *Lower, dim, gigantic, in the night.*
> > *Where is the way?*
>
> *I'm standing Lord:*
> *The black rock hems me in behind,*
> *Above my head a moaning wind*
> *Chills and oppresses heart and mind.*
> > *I am afraid!*
>
> *I'm standing, Lord:*
> *The rock is hard beneath my feet;*
> *I nearly slipped, Lord, on the sleet.*
> *So weary, Lord! And where a seat?*
> > *Still must I stand?*

He answered me, and on His face
A look ineffable of grace,
Of perfect, understanding love,
Which all my murmuring did remove.

I'm standing, Lord:
Since Thou hast spoken, Lord, I see
Thou hast beset—these rocks are Thee!
And since Thy love encloses me,
I stand and sing.

Betty was able to flourish in her talents both in childhood and while at school. The time spent as a missionary child with a unique perspective of the world ultimately would prepare her for her future in ministry.

Betty Scott's Surrender

October 7, 1926

Dearest little sister Bunny,

Let's make the Pacific Ocean narrower, and the continent of America, too, this year, by being in closer touch with each other. Let's tell each other things that we are especially interested in, and not let time and distance apart stop our being real sisters. I love you, dear, more than I ever did when we were all at home together, and I know that in the future we will all be the best of chums together. You see, since I've been away from home, I've learned to trust the Lord better, with the result that I begin to understand what trust really means; that one gets the power and the inspiration to love more faithfully and more unselfishly. The result is that, instead of making a good time and lots of attention and many compliments the height of my ambition, I have now let the Lord take charge of my life and put His will and His glory first. And, Bunny, it does away with that awful, dissatisfied feeling that used to be so close that it was always sticking around and preparing to nab me. Of course, there are times now when I forget for a moment that I am the Lord's and then my horrible old self rages around and makes herself very conspicuous.

Now you can see by this paper heading (which, by the way, is not strictly meant for letter writing in general, but only for business notes), that I am one of the officers of the Student Volunteer Union of this part of the country. That means that I am one of a large number of college boys and girls who have decided that the missionary life is the life for them, and that, if nothing else comes up which seems to be God's particular will for them, they will most certainly end by going out as missionaries under some foreign board.

It has taken me some time to decide that I wanted to be a missionary, and the main reason against my finally deciding was this: the fact that I am a missionary's daughter and that everyone just naturally expects me to do the same thing, missionary work, myself. You understand what I mean, don't you, honey? One naturally hates to do what people expect one to; and the feeling that you ought to do a thing doesn't help you much, either. In fact, I found it true that there was a different way to go at the thing. Instead of saying, "Oh dear, why do I have to do it, just because other people want me to? I won't!" Then, "Oh, I know that no one will be happy until I do as I'm supposed to. I feel that something is just forcing me to do it, and I don't want to. I don't! I won't!--Why do I have to?" (You see what I mean?)

Well, I began by trying to trust in the Lord, and in saying something like this: "Lord, I'm not a bit happy, going on the way I am. I want people to like me, and sometimes they do, and sometimes they don't. Please tell me how to be happy!"

Then He seemed to say: "How can I help you, child? You are
fighting against Me with all your might. It isn't My way
to force people to do things; they must tell me that I am
welcome before I can do very much with their lives."

Then I said, "I suppose that You want me to give up all the
things that are fun, and be a stupid old maid missionary,
with thick and stubby black shoes and a tight-waisted
white dress!"

But He only said, "I only want your love and obedience," and
that made me mad, and very uncomfortable. So it went on.

Then in desperation I said, "What will You give me, if I
simply give over everything to You? Maybe I'll be sorry."

Then He said: "What you get depends on how much you give.
And don't you think that the experiment is worth trying?"

Well, I can't remember all the details of the fight; but,
believe me, it was a battle royal, all right. And all the
time I was getting more and more desperate. Finally, I
said--Oh, I know it must have been the last stand for
Satan, for it was perfectly terrible--"Well, I'll never be
happy this way, so You might just as well have Your own way,
Jesus. Here, take me," and I practically threw myself at
Him. Immediately, I had the most terrible feeling. I nearly
died of sorrow. I thought, "Is this how I have been talking
to God?" and I cried so hard that I could hardly breathe. I
felt like crawling under the lowest and dirtiest floor and
waiting there to be struck by lightning.

But, you see, I was really humble by that time. And I
guess that that was what Christ was trying to accomplish;
He couldn't do a thing with me while I was all puffed
up. Then, He wouldn't let me stay groveling in the dirt
anymore; but He was wonderfully kind and sympathetic and
encouraging, and as I kept on sobbing, "Oh, forgive me!

forgive me!" He said very clearly, "I have forgiven you. Now I have taken the rubbish out of your heart, too. Do you want Me to come and stay, instead?"

"Oh yes, dear Lord," I said, and I knew that was what I'd been wanting all my life, and never knew it! And almost the first thing I said then, was: "What can I do for Thee, Jesus? I give Thee all I have, and I hope that Thou canst use me, although there is nothing good in me!"

And He said, "Do you remember the five loaves and two fishes? What is given to Me I can bless, so that the good it does cannot be measured. All I want is a perfectly whole heart, no matter how unattractive and sin-stained the person who owns it."

"Mine is Yours, O Lord," I said, and I felt as though, if I opened my eyes, I should see the Holy Spirit descending in flames of fire on the heads of people around and on me. Suddenly I started in thrilled surprise. "Oh, I know what You want me to do! Be a missionary! I will, if You will help me and go with me all the way."

And now you see why I am a Student Volunteer, and why I think that anyone who tries to force himself to be a missionary (or anything else) is putting the cart before the horse and has probably not spoken with God on the subject at all.

Best of love, dear Bunny, and I shall certainly write you again soon.

Your loving sister,

Betty

CHAPTER FIVE

Together at Moody

As the 1920s came to an end, Moody Bible Institute had already established itself as one of the premiere Christian institutions in the world, with James M. Gray serving as its president since 1904. Founded in 1886 on the Near North Side of Chicago by Dwight L. Moody, it was Moody's vision to equip and train Christian workers with the gifts God granted them to further proclaim the gospel.

When John entered that fall of 1929, his heart and mind were completely set on his studies. He first enrolled in the Missionary Course, which included training in several ministry subjects. Sensing a need for further knowledge of the Scriptures, John transferred a year later to the General Bible Course. At the time, Moody did not grant a bachelor's degree; rather a diploma was given after a student's three-year program study in their desired field.

The secretary of the school would later write of John: "He had the bearing and mind of a college or university-trained man. He was well balanced and energetic, possessing good judgment and considerable initiative. In his Practical Christian Work he proved to be a good speaker and an exceptionally good group leader."

One faculty member stated of John, "He will undoubtedly be heard from." Another predicted, "Expect to see this young man make good in a large way." Fellow students thought highly of John and his unwavering lifestyle, while admiring the down-to-earth approach he took in the Christian faith.

Several prayer meetings were part of Moody Bible Institute's extracurricular to engage students in the impact of global ministry. One of these was for the China Inland Mission, held on Monday evenings at the Chicago home of

Dr. Isaac Page and his wife, Isabella, who were the mission representatives for the Midwest.

Betty attended the meetings regularly since starting Moody, for by then her call to the country was nearly unmistakable. John soon found himself among the China bunch, as they were often referred to. After the meetings, refreshments were served, and Dr. Page might introduce some of his favorite books to the students. One of these many texts presented was *Letters of the Rev. Samuel Rutherford.* Knowing these words were already precious to John, Dr. Page reflected on two lives being bound in that moment: "Never shall I forget the look in Betty Scott's eyes as I repeated those wonderful verses on Immanuel's Land." John was open to the prospect of serving overseas should the Lord direct him. He was raised in a home where missions work was strongly supported and discussed. One of his older brothers, Harry, was already a missionary with his family to the Belgian Congo of Africa.

By June 1930, a tense civil war exploded in China. Two years earlier, the National Revolutionary Army (military arm of the Chinese Nationalist Party) had defeated a coalition of local warlords and temporarily reunited China under a new nationalist government, led by Chiang Kai-shek. The tenuous alliance collapsed when Chiang killed thousands of communists and leftist rebels (the Shanghai Massacre). The Chinese Communist Party responded in a series of rebel disturbances in Nanchang, led by factional forces known as the Chinese Red Army. The Chinese would later call this the "Ten Year Civil War," and the damage to missionary efforts was incalculable.

The communists regarded the Christian religion as the superstitious propaganda of foreign imperialism. Due to America's support of the Nationalist Party and Chiang Kai-shek, the communists believed there was no worse enemy than a Western missionary to the country. The communist strategy was to kidnap missionaries and hold them hostage for large ransoms, attempting to bleed the Americans financially and force them to leave China.

While the tactic seemed simple on paper, almost every Christian missionary in the country knew a ransom would never be paid, and this so-called strategy proved time and time again to fail. As time progressed, killing American hostages became a new means of intimidation and new pressure on the American government to stay out of Chinese politics.

Three associates of CIM had already suffered death at the hands of these rebel bandits, and two others were still being held in captivity. Of this situation John wrote to a brother:

> It is an amazing thing that the provinces in China which are having most trouble are the very provinces in which the China Inland Mission has, after prayerful consideration, decided to press forward with evangelistic efforts. Two of their most valued workers, Mr. and Mrs. R. W. Porteous, are still in the hands of bandits, but reports have come through that they are teaching and preaching among their captors. It is said that the Communist soldiers like them so well that they declare that "these old people are too good to kill." They wish they would become Communists! With all its internal troubles, there seem to be unparalleled opportunities in China.

The very next day after John wrote those words, the Porteouses were released. Their captivity lasted exactly one hundred days.

When John went to Moody, he saved some money to help pay for his first year's tuition as well as room and board. His family knew he was not financially stable at the time, but figured John would reach out to them as soon as his funds depleted. This, however, was not the case. Reminded that serving God was a faithful endeavor, John looked to the Lord to provide for his needs, trusting Him to supply. John held a part-time job waiting tables in the Institute's cafeteria, and while it didn't meet all his financial needs, he diligently served others around campus out of good spirit. As these notions were in mind, he reported to his brother Harry:

> The Lord has wonderfully taken care of me all through my stay here at Moody's. I count it a great privilege to be here, if only for the lessons I have learned of Him and His dealings with men. . . . The classroom work is blessed, but I think I have learned even more outside of classes than in them.

In January 1931, John started traveling two hundred miles outside Chicago to Elida, Ohio, where he began an interim pastor role for a small country church. It was not always an easy journey for John, especially during the winter months, but what he brought to the community of believers cultivated a lasting effect.

"John was more than our minister," shared one congregant. "He not only taught and preached, he was our close and intimate friend also. He visited most if not all of us in our homes. He was quick to see a joke, and could be jolly and enjoy himself wherever he happened to be, especially where there were young folks and children. And they loved him greatly."

When preaching, he passionately dwelled on the theme of faithfulness in his sermons, both the faithfulness in the Christian life and God's own to His people. Among John's favorite verses were these two:

> Thou wilt keep him in perfect peace, whose mind is stayed on thee: because he trusteth in thee. (Isa. 26:3)

> So that we may boldly say, The Lord is my helper, and I will not fear what man shall do unto me. (Heb. 13:6)

Numerous missionary speakers and pastors provided a great impact on John's exploration of faith and ministry call. As he read various prayer letters from around the world, his heart widened for the need to spread the gospel to the mostly unevangelized parts of the globe. Even with this desire, John became weary of exactly where God was leading. His father, who was getting older in age, was hoping his son would return from Moody to take up the work at the Star of Hope back in Paterson. John regularly spoke at the family mission while on school breaks and during the summer, but he still felt unsure about a definitive calling.

He wrote to his brother Jacob about the matter:

> The Lord knows where He wants me, whether in Holland, in Paterson or some other place in the States, in China, or in India. However, it does look frightfully disproportionate to see so many here in comparison with the few over yonder. We know that the Lord's work is not overstaffed here, but, as someone has said, "There are those who simply cannot go and those who are free to go. Why should both stay at home for the same work?"

During his second year at Moody, another pressing situation was his deepening relationship with Betty Scott. John and Betty's association started as a close friendship. They often worked together at ministry events around

Chicago and spent time together during the China prayer meetings. Out of this developed a mutual romantic attraction between their closely guarded hearts. Betty was drawn to John's tall figure and mature outgoing personality. John saw in Betty a Christ-centered heart for missionary work. Both also had multiple siblings and shared a strong family trait of wanting to spread the gospel among the unsaved. But even as they complemented each other, both understood that if they were directed to different fields of service, the two would not sustain a long-term relationship.

Several years earlier, shortly before starting at Wilson College, Betty wrote a poem titled "My Ideal" in which she described the characteristics and traits she would look for in a potential spouse:

My Ideal

I'll recognize my true love
When once his face I see;
For he will strong and healthy,
And broad of shoulder be:
His movements will be agile,
And quick, and full of grace;
The eyes of Galahad will smile
In his so friendly face.

His features won't be Grecian,
Nor yet will they be rough;
His fingers will be flexible,
Long, and strong and tough:
Oh, he'll be tall, and active
As any Indian,
With rounded muscles rippling out
Beneath his healthy tan.

He will not be a smoker,
A drinker, nor a cheat;
He'll know the art of tongue-control;
He'll know how much to eat;

He will not be a dandy,
  "Society" he loathes,
Nor yet will he be awkward
  In spotless evening clothes.

He may be literary,
  I hope, mechanical;
But of one thing I'm certain;
  His voice is musical,
His common sense is excellent,
  Basically sound;
And cool in any crisis
  His judgment will be found.

His interest is boundless
  In every fellow man;
He'll gladly be a champion
  As often as he can:
Oh, he'll be democratic,
  And maybe shock the prude,
He will not fawn before the great,
  Nor to the low be rude.

He'll be a splendid "mixer,"
  For he has sympathy,
Perhaps his most pronounced trait
  Is versatility;
If Providence should drop him
  In any foreign town,
He'd somehow speak the language
  And find his way around.

He'll have a sense of humor
  As kindly as it's keen;
Somehow, though never spendthrift,
  He's also never mean;

His patience and unselfishness
  May readily be seen;
He's very fond of children,
  And children worship him.

He will not be a rich man
  He has no earthly hoard;
His money, time, heart, mind, and soul
  Are given to the Lord.
Oh, if he ever finds me,
  My answer "Yes" will be;
For I could trust and cherish
  Him, to eternity!

Betty realized that John seemed a good fit of her articulate description. She wondered if, in fact, he might be the one God had planned for her. This mindful notion soon came to a pause. As months passed in the spring of 1931 and Betty was to graduate before John, both sensed—independently of each other—that God was leading them toward service in China, possibly with CIM.

As a result of the Chinese Civil War starting in 1927, thousands of people in the country were left dead. Roughly half of all foreign missionaries vacated, never to return. Half of the missionaries with CIM were forced to temporarily leave their stations, disappointing many families both at home and those being helped abroad.

In March 1929, Dixon Hoste, general director of the CIM, sent out a call for two hundred or more workers in the next two years to take up the cause. Labeled the *forward movement*, this challenge greatly stirred John's soul. He wrote to a brother about this passion in his life, which seemed more urgent as time went on: "A million a month pass into Christless graves over there. God can use us if only we are empty, broken vessels in His hand. Oh, how much more do we need preparation of heart and spirit than of the mind! Pray that I may have that."

Betty Scott was one of the women who responded to the appeal and made her application with CIM during her final year. She was to attend their candidate school in the Germantown neighborhood of Philadelphia, Pennsylvania, following graduation. John's heart for this period soon became fully devoted to God. He not only planned to go to China unmarried but to remain so for at least five years. He was never one to keep a woman from her own ambitions, even back home in Paterson, and since he had another year at Moody, he held out on committing to Betty. He hoped to join CIM after his last year, but was still required to pass a medical test and be accepted by the director and council.

The CIM application screening process was a daunting task. One not only had to be physically and spiritually capable but also mentally sound for the frequent disturbances. If the individual felt led to apply, they first filled out an application in which they were asked to write a spiritual autobiography, doctrinal statement, and sense of calling in life. The applicant was also asked to provide three references, who were each asked to provide three more references. This vigorous screening allowed the mission to help determine background and character.

In April 1931, Betty graduated from Moody with a diploma in the Medical Missionary Service Course and left Chicago for Philadelphia. While studying that summer at candidate school, Betty spent time seeing her family friends, the Howards, who ran *The Sunday School Times*. Phillip E. Howard Jr. had returned to the States four years prior after serving in Belgium as a missionary with his wife, Katharine, and settled in the Germantown neighborhood. The Howards' oldest child, also named Elisabeth, remembered as a four-year-old sitting at the dinner table of their duplex home on May 11, 1931, hearing Betty Scott share her testimony with the family. Betty's life prayer, written at the age of nineteen while at Keswick, made a profound impression on Elisabeth Howard, and she later went on to make the expression of faith her own after discovering it at the age of twelve. The full prayer reads:

> Lord, I give up my own plans and purposes, all my own desires, hopes and ambitions, and I accept Thy will for my life. I give up myself, my life, my all, utterly to Thee, to be Thine forever. I hand over to Thy keeping all of my friendships; all the people whom I love are to take second place in my heart. Fill me now and seal me with Thy Spirit. Work out Thy whole will in my life at any cost, for to me to live is Christ. Amen.

John desired to correspond with Betty via mail while separated but was uneasy about his motivations of pursuing her along with his own ambitions of becoming a missionary. The two still maintained strong feelings for each other. On May 24, he recorded in his diary the internal conflict within him:

Betty is in Philadelphia now, but I have not been able to write her a letter. After much searching of heart and of the Scriptures, I feel that the Lord would be displeased at my going forward in this direction. And only last week a man came up to my room to have me type a letter for him. A former student, he told me with tears in his eyes that he had gotten out of the will of the Lord when he stopped his studies and got married. What grief he has had since. And now, while Betty and I are looking forward to the same field, I cannot move one step in her direction until I am sure that it is the Lord's directive will. I don't want to wreck her life and mine too.

Charles and Clara Scott came back to America on furlough that summer, so with their five children, the family vacationed the months of July and August in Ventnor, New Jersey. This marked the last time all the siblings were together.

Meanwhile, as John was to begin his final year at Moody, he set his mind on studies and preparing for what lay ahead. Before heading back for Chicago that fall, he served as best man at his brother Neil's wedding to Henrietta Winter on September 1, at the Star of Hope Mission. He was delighted to share this moment with his younger brother in the same building where the Lord convicted them nearly a full decade earlier. A few weeks later, John wrote to his parents, revealing his own thoughts and intentions regarding Betty:

Since I still feel the Lord would have me spend some time alone, I told Betty that in all fairness and love to her, I could not and would not ask her to enter into an engagement with years to wait. But we can have a real understanding and thus be free to let the interests of the Lord's work always be first.

The CIM has appealed for men, single men, to do itinerating work out in sections where it would be in some cases almost impossible to travel with women, and at least they feel it unfair to take women up into these unsettled sections until at a work has been started. After a work has been started, we all recognize that women are needed. You can't reach the native women any other way. But they are looking for men to travel from village preaching and distributing literature. The men at the head of the mission are seasoned missionaries, men of God, and are fully aware of the dangers and trials on the field, and yet they feel that what they need is single men for this work. Some time ago I promised the Lord that if I was fitted for that work, I would gladly go, and so now I feel that I cannot back down without a very good reason, reasons that would show the work of the Lord could be advanced by my changing my course, not merely reasons that concern personal convenience. Apostolic example seems to point to that way, and I suppose that really ought to be our first reason.

And now, Dad and Mother, from the way I've written this you'd think I was talking about a carload of lumber I was negotiating for, instead of something that has dug down deep into our hearts. Both Betty and I have been praying very much about this, and I know you have too, and of this I am sure, if we are foolishly waiting, and the Lord's work will not be really prospered by our waiting, truly the Lord will not let us miss out on any of His blessings if our hearts are set to do His will show us.

But this is true, isn't it, that our wishes must not come first. The progress of the Lord's work is to be the first consideration. And so, there are times when we just have to stop and think hard.

Betty was accepted on September 16 for service and visited the Howard family again on the 30th along with her parents. In early October, Betty made her way cross-country, stopping in Chicago to see John before departing. They two spent hours together down by Lake Michigan to talk and pray, as both knew it might be the last chance they would get to see each other for years. The day coincidentally happened to be a Monday, so that evening John and Betty attended the China prayer meeting that first brought them together. Dr. Page recalled of that night:

When it was over they wanted to talk with me, and John, in a very delightful way, tried to tell me what was in his heart regarding Betty. He thought we had not noticed anything! Then, speaking for both of them, he said that they were leaving the matter in the Lord's hands, but felt that He was bringing them together.

Betty proceeded to the West Coast before sailing for China on October 15. Giving an update to supporters, her picture and a brief testimony appeared in that November's issue of *China's Millions*, CIM's official magazine:

> A Missionary's daughter, brought up in China, I have always seen something of heathenism. But, although I knew the Lord as my Savior so early that I cannot remember any definite decision, many experiences and battles followed before I truly accepted the Savior as my Lord.
>
> During school years, I prayed that if it were God's will nothing might prevent me from returning to China as a missionary. My parents and others prayed thus about me, too. I, myself, first made this prayer in 1925 at Keswick, where I received this verse, "To me to live is Christ, and to die is gain." Since then, other lines of activity, even other fields, have come up before me—and I cannot say they were not of the Lord—while even as late as September, this year, it was uncertain whether, for physical reasons, I would be accepted at all.
>
> But, I, being in the way, the Lord led me. He, who made me willing to serve Him anywhere, has closed all other doors and opened this one—service under the China Inland Mission in China. For this I praise His name; for I love China and believe it is the neediest country—just now, more so than ever. I will make mention of His faithfulness, which is great. Praising the Lord is, I believe, the only thing in the world worth doing. And praising Him involves bringing other members of His body—those now in heathenism—to Him.

CHAPTER SIX

Pressing Onward

Shortly after Betty arrived in China, she began language school with a group of women in the city of Yangchow (Yangzhou today), located in the central Jiangsu Province. She was delighted to discover that much of the language learned as a child was easy to pick up again and made significant progress the next several months studying.

John diligently continued in the opportunities ministering both in Chicago and Elida. His heart and conscience increasingly became burdened for the non-Christian world during those final months of study. Before the school year ended, two reminders of God's faithful provision were shown. The first of these involved a blue suit John's brother Jacob had given him the prior year to pass along to another student at Moody who could use it. For months he had looked for a young man who might be able to benefit from the suit but couldn't seem to find one. Just as John had thought about giving the suit away to a mission, he saw a student in fellowship who he heard wasn't well off financially. Finding the student alone downstairs, John presented him with the suit. The lad told John that he had just begun to pray for a suit earlier that day. "Of course it fits him!" John noted in his diary that evening.

By the middle of April, only a few days before his graduation, John found himself once again short on funds. That morning on the way to pick up his own suit that was recently pressed by a tailor, he stopped at the campus post office to retrieve his mail. John eagerly checked the multiple letters he had gotten to see if there was any money. Realizing there was none, he went back to the tailor and asked if he would wait for the sixty cents that was due. John then remembered a package he picked up earlier from the post office. Figuring the package contained no money, John didn't bother to open it, but upon doing so he discovered a single dollar among the other contents. With this he had enough to pay for the repair of the suit and get a needed haircut for the upcoming ceremony. That night he wrote, "I won't have a new suit for graduation, but I'll have the Lord's grace instead, and that's enough! Hallelujah! The Lord certainly has helped me in this very, very busy time."

Three days later, on April 21, 1932, John's class held their graduation exercises. John had the distinguished honor of being selected as the male representative to speak from his class to address the graduates and hundreds of guests who attended the ceremony. Seventy-three students graduated, fifty-one of whom anticipated Christian vocation service in America and several foreign countries. Their eagerness to serve was reflected in the class motto, "Bearing Precious Seed," based on Psalm 126:6. John's address, titled "Go Forward!" was a courageous challenge to advance the cause of Christ both at home and abroad to those who otherwise wouldn't know the gospel. For print on his graduation photo, he chose the verse Lamentations 3:22–23: "It is of the LORD's mercies that we are not consumed, because his compassions fail not. They are new every morning; great is thy faithfulness."

After a six-week stay at the home of CIM in Philadelphia following graduation, John was approved for missionary service on July 1, 1932. The prospect of a marriage proposal to Betty was heavily on his mind. A diary entry the day before being accepted reveals his fervor in committing himself to the Lord's calling.

> It seems to me that I have been looking too much for some supernatural guidance. It is hard to describe one's feelings, and yet I do have a sense that I am in the way. I have prayed much about this, perhaps more than about any one single thing ever in my life. I have studied my Bible for guidance, and can see no hindrance there at all, if not positive guidance. And circumstances more than point in that direction. May God frustrate everything if it is not of Him. I do want His will first.

John stayed with his family in Paterson the remainder of that summer and committed his last months to the Star of Hope Mission. He was invited to go on a "Revelation Cruise" with other Christian friends which was to tour Bermuda and other unique sites, but ultimately declined. John thought it might be misunderstood with his desire set on the less fortunate that he should partake in such a luxurious experience.

In early August, he wrote Betty asking for her consent to marry him someday. John felt justified in doing this after much prayer and because they both were led to serve under the same mission organization.

A going away service was held at the mission the night of September 3, with Dr. Robert H. Glover, North American director of CIM, preaching on Paul's attitude toward the missionary cause. John also gave his personal testimony. Many friends in the community as well as members of the Stam family gathered to share in the joyous occasion. The next day John was the main preacher in the afternoon Sunday school and spoke again in the evening with the head of the candidate school. On September 5, John signed his "last will and testament" in the event of his death in China, with his brother Jacob, now an established lawyer in Paterson, overlooking as executor. John listed Betty as the one to inherit his estate even knowing he might not see her immediately overseas. As witnesses to the signing and next in line to the estate were two of his brothers, Henry and Cornelius, and then Dow Brain (fiancé of John's younger sister Amelia).

On Tuesday, September 6, about forty people gathered at the train station in Paterson to see John off with singing and prayer. He would spend the next two weeks traveling across British Columbia and part of the United States to speak a few more times before leaving for China. He'd travel by rail from Toronto to Vancouver, British Columbia, where he was to depart. Along the way he received a letter from Betty. To his surprise, she hadn't heard any word from him, including the marriage proposal he wrote a few weeks earlier.

In recent months, Betty had gone through a series of despairing circumstances. Henry Ferguson, a missionary to China for thirty-seven years, had been captured by communist rebels in northern Anhwei Province on May 12. Since he was never seen or heard from again, it was presumed he had been killed. Consequently, Betty and other female missionaries in that area of the province were temporarily moved to the CIM station in Wuhu. Her parents wrote requesting that Betty meet them in Shanghai when they returned in early fall from their furlough. Arriving at the requested time, to her disappointment she found out their trip had been delayed. She had not received the message that their trip was postponed to a later date, and eventually discovering that, went back to Wuhu. In addition to all this, Betty questioned why she had not heard from John for quite some time.

While traveling John wrote in his diary on September 22:

> Have had a blessed time coming across the continent. The trip through the Rockies was specially interesting and I couldn't help but praise God again for all His great goodness—Yesterday I received a letter from Betty, not the one I expected though—The poor girl was in Shanghai and hadn't heard from me for some time. Mr. Stark had told her I was accepted and asked if I was still interested—I do hope my letter gets through to her—However the will of the Lord be done—I have no goal and no desire beyond Him—But I do believe that He will give me Betty on the way.

Even with his heart's ambition for Betty, John knew the high priority of serving. A friend later said of spending one of those final days in America with him:

> When I last saw John, we went upon Garret Mountain which overlooks Paterson, our hometown. One can see practically the entire city, besides New York, Newark, and nearer places. I thought by his silence that he was taking it all in, but his thoughts were far away. "Just think, Tom," he said at length, "that there are scores of cities in China, as large as this one, in which they do not have the gospel."

John C. Stam

John C. Stam
Rescued from the Loot

Tsing'teh China
Dec. 1934

Cornelius R. Stam

Stam family, 1917: (top) Clazina, Harry, Henry, Jacob, Peter Stam Jr.;
(bottom) Neil, Amelia Sr., Amelia, Peter Stam Sr., Margaret (wife of Peter Jr.), John

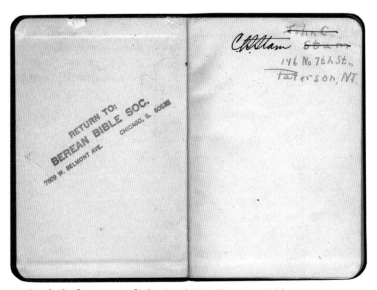

Inside the front cover of John Stam's New Testament Bible as a teenager

Star of Hope Mission postcard, 1920s

PETER STAM AND STAFF
STAR OF HOPE MISSION
PATERSON, NEW JERSEY
(1920)

Star of Hope Mission staff, 1920 (Wheaton Archives)

Stam family, mid-1920s: John (top left), Neil (top right)

Stam brothers, 1923: (from left)
Jacob, Neil, Henry, John, Harry

Sailing, 1928: John (top left),
Henry (at wheel)

Family sailing, 1928: John (bottom left), Neil (top right)

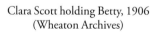

Extended Stam family, Thanksgiving Day 1928: Neil and John (top center)

Clara Scott holding Betty, 1906
(Wheaton Archives)

Betty and Helen Scott, 1916
(Wheaton Archives)

Scott family postcard, 1916
(Wheaton Archives)

Scott family, January 1, 1918: (from left; top) Betty, Helen; (bottom) Beatrice, Charles, Kenneth, Clara, Francis (Wheaton Archives)

Inside the front cover of *Scarlet and Purple* by Sydney Watson, which Betty was reading at the Keswick Conference

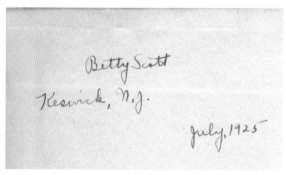

Betty Scott
Keswick, N.J.
July, 1925

Betty's senior yearbook photo
from Wilson College, 1928

Literary Society staff at Wilson College, 1928:
Betty sitting on couch (left); Marguerite Luce (top row, third from left)

Dr. Isaac Page (Wheaton Archives)

Isabella Page (Wheaton Archives)

Girls from Moody China prayer group, spring 1931:
Betty (second from left), Isaac Page in middle (Wheaton Archives)

Moody China group, spring 1931 (Wheaton Archives)

Students outside Ransom Hall, spring 1931: John Stam at front center sitting on shoulders of friend Otto Schoerner (Wheaton Archives)

Studying for final exams, spring 1931: John Stam (far right) (Wheaton Archives)

CIM training home in Philadelphia, summer 1931 (Wheaton Archives)

Women at CIM home, summer 1931: Betty (top right), Katie Dodd (bottom right)
(Wheaton Archives)

Christmas card from John to Moody classmate Marguerite Goodner, early 1930s (Wheaton Archives)

Last complete Scott family photo, taken in Ventnor, New Jersey, August 1931:
(top) Charles Scott, Marianne Hirst (best friend of Helen), Helen, Kenneth, Francis;
(bottom) Beatrice, Betty, Clara Scott (Wheaton Archives)

Missionary Union Executives, April 11, 1932: John Stam (far left) (Wheaton Archives)

John on roof of building 152
at Moody, April 11, 1932
(Wheaton Archives)

John's Moody graduation photo, spring 1932

John Stam's Graduation Speech
"Go Forward!"

Moody Bible Institute of Chicago, April 21, 1932

Dr. Gray, Members of the Faculty, Classmates, Fellow students, and friends:

Under the good hand of God we were led to come to the Moody Bible Institute two years or more ago, impelled by the desire to equip ourselves more fully for the service of our Lord. We do thank God for this place and for the lessons we have learned here, and grasp this opportunity to express our gratitude to everyone who has helped to make our training here a possibility, and especially to those under whose faithful ministry we have grown in the knowledge of our Lord.

Friendships have been made here which have already been and will forever be a source of rich blessing, and this morning our hearts beat a bit more quickly as we realize that this particular section of what has so often been called our "Institute Family" will never meet again as we do today until we meet at the feet of our blessed Lord. But now as we turn our thoughts from the associations of this place toward the work for which we have been preparing, there is borne in upon us the great challenge of the task that is ours. In the audience seated before me there are many men and women engaged in some form of Christian activity beside our present student body now in training for the work of the Lord. To you, my friends, and to the church of Christ at large, as well as to us come the same challenge of an unsown field awaiting those who bear the precious seed.

Our Lord told us that the field is the world. In politics today me are thinking in terms of international affairs, in business all the continents are being combed for markets, and even in daily life every newspaper reader is becoming world-conscious. And yet we, the people of God, have not fully realized that we are to be a testimony to the world. We say that the door of heaven is shut to everyone who does not come through Christ, and while millions are dying without having heard His name, we are shamefully cold and indifferent toward foreign mission work. Heathen populations are growing in numbers daily, but we are not reaching them, much less matching their increasing

numbers with increased efforts to bring them the gospel. Not only are heathen populations growing, but with the frontiers of civilization forging ahead
and education advancing, superstition and idolatry are breaking down. Now
is the time as never before to reach men whose minds are swept of old barriers
ere Communistic Atheism coming in like a flood raises other barriers tenfold
harder to level, and before this generation of heathen passes into Christless
graves. Our answer last year to this challenge of the pagan millions was less
than two cents a week for foreign missions from the average Protestants in
the United States, and this year we are giving even less.

Our own civilized land also challenges us today as Christian workers. This
country once so strong in its Christian testimony is becoming increasingly
godless. Our educational systems are taking us away from God. The old
standards of morality are fast going, and those great and holy truths once so
sacred are becoming the butt of jokes to furnish humor for our periodicals.
Here and there we do see a bright testimony to the truth of God, but as a
whole those who do know the truth as it is in Christ Jesus are not answering
the challenge of the day by preaching it as it should be preached.

If the foreign field and the godless civilization about us both call for the
faithful planting of divine dynamite that will break stony hearts and save
souls, the church of Christ surely has a claim upon our service. I am thinking now of that section of the Protestant church which we call conservative
and fundamental, those who would rise up in quick denial should they be
called modernistic, —our own people. We have not that abounding life,
and we seem to have lost that happy spirit of fellowship with one another,
and of joy in God which ought to make us an attraction to the unsaved. Our
prayer meetings have lost the place and the power they once had, and many
of our people know not the joy of winning others for the Lord. Instead of
reaching out for the unsaved, great numbers of our churches are not holding
what they have. Complaints are being made about the deadness and lack
of interest among our church members. They tell us that our young people
who have been brought up in the church are hard to hold. But is it any wonder? How can a dead and dry orthodoxy, lacking the joy and power of true
Christianity, ever hope to hold its own? We have been guilty of acting more
like the beleaguered garrison of a doomed fortress than like the soldiers of

our Conquering Christ. Surely our churches call for men and women to faithfully labour in the word and doctrine.

Such is the challenge of the task that is ours. The heathen world, and civilized world, and the church of Christ all look to us and inquire, "What will you do about such conditions?" If there is a challenge in the work itself, the difficulties under which the work must be done are equally challenging. We do thank God for those who are looking upward, and in times like these planning new advances into enemy territory, but large sections of the lines are falling back. Supplies are not coming up from the rear, contributions are falling off, and worst of all, the spirit of aggression is gone. We are not tremendously upset to see missionaries returning for lack of funds, and volunteers unable to go forward for the same reason. It does not pain us to realize that light is being denied those who sit in darkness and in the shadow of death. All forms of Christian work at home and abroad are quite naturally feeling the effect of the Depression, but we have not risen to the occasion and demonstrated to this world that God's people at home as well as on the field can sacrifice joyfully to keep His work going forward. As Christian workers, what attitude shall we take, and what shall we do with income falling and conditions seemingly impossible? We dare not resort to methods unworthy of our Master to raise funds for His work. Shall we beat a retreat and turn back from our high calling in Christ Jesus? Or dare we advance at God's command in the face of the impossible?

Moses at the Red Sea faced just such a condition as we face today. His people were to be a testimony for the One True God to the heathen tribes of the earth. Civilized Egypt from which God had delivered them by His mighty power seemed about to overwhelm them. They were weak in resources for they were soon to come to the very last of their provisions. But worst of all was the spirit of the people. They had ceased to look forward to victory, were murmuring and complaining, and in their hearts they still preferred the settled state of bondage in Egypt to venturing out on the faithfulness of their Mighty God. For the moment they had lost the sense of His presence and of His mighty power. In such a crisis, with everything against him, Moses could do only one thing. He prayed. Though his prayer is unrecorded, we read that the answer is swift and emphatic, "Wherefore criest thou unto me, Speak unto the people that they go forward."

Today as in Moses' day, the hosts of darkness would shout with glee to see the testimony of God hindered in foreign lands. Our Egypt, that godless civilization from which we have been saved by mighty power, would gladly reclaim us as the slaves of sin. Our supplies seem so inadequate, and our people too have ceased to look forward to the victory. What shall we do? Surely we can follow Moses' example to great profit, —we can pray. And what think you will the answer be? Will our God who once commanded us to preach the gospel to every nation order a retreat because conditions seem impossible? Let us remind ourselves that the Great Commission was never qualified by clauses that called for advance only if funds were plentiful and if no hardship or self-denial were involved. On the contrary, we were told to expect tribulation and even persecution, but with it victory in Christ. Surely His answer today is just what was in Moses' day, "Speak unto the people that they go forward."

Friends, the challenge of our task with all its attendant difficulties is enough to full our hearts with dismay, and if we look only to ourselves and to our weakness, we are overcome with forebodings of defeat. But the answering challenge in our Master's command to go forward should full us with joy and with the expectation of victory. He knows our weakness and our lack of supplies; He knows the roughness of the way, and His command carries with it the assurance of all we need for the work. Of course we want to be assured of our support! Who cares to go forward in any enterprise, secular or religious, unless he can be reasonably sure that it will not have to be dropped for lack of funds? But let us remind ourselves that even in the business world there is nothing at all sure. Incomes are falling, men are losing employment, and bank accounts are being wiped out. Do we, as Christian workers, want to be sure of support? Then let us not put our trust in men, or in any God-dishonoring methods of raising funds for the work. These are not certain enough. We have it on the highest authority that the promise is of FAITH that it might be sure. The faithfulness of God is the only certain thing in the world today and we need not fear the result of trusting Him.

Our way is plain. We must not retrench in any work which we are convinced is in His will and for His glory. We dare not turn back because the way looks dark. Classmates, some of us may be called of God to be Christian business-men, but may God grant that none of us, called of Him for full-time gospel ministry, may forget His call and turn back to secular work because we are afraid support will be lacking. Of this we may be sure, that if we have been redeemed by Christ's blood, and are called into His service, His work done in His way and for His glory will never lack His support. We must go forward in the face of the impossible even if we know only the next step. We have often sung,

I do not ask to see the distant scene,
One step enough for me.

Did we mean it? Then let us suit our actions to our songs and we shall find that

New supplies each hour I meet,
While travelling on to God.

We may find ourselves at the place where we shall have to drink the bitter waters of Marah, but our Captain's presence can sweeten even bitter water. We may come to the very last bit of our provisions with starvation staring us in the face, but He is still able to give us each day our daily bread. And what if we should, like Allen Gardener, die of starvation in the fight? Like him we shall find our moments of suffering aglow with the sunshine of Christ's presence, and we shall have nothing but praise for the grace and mercy bestowed upon us. We dare go forward, sure that "He is able to make all grace abound to us that we always having all sufficiency in all things may abound to every good work."

Some of us will be called of God to labor in our churches at home, and in answering that challenge we must teach our people anew the joy of walking with God, and of witnessing for Him. Let us show them how to sacrifice joyfully for His work, so that in these hard times, the world may see how, that in a great trial of affliction, the abundance of our joy, yes, and perhaps even our deep poverty may abound unto the riches of liberality in supporting the work of God.

And whether we labor in the churches, or in evangelistic work, or in missions, we must all seek to answer the cry of this godless civilization by turning men to Him who saves from the penalty and power of sin. This bewildered age needs to know that only the foundation of God standeth sure.

God is using these days to tear many a man loose from the things to which his heart has clung. It is ours to show them incorruptible riches which bank failures and economic conditions cannot touch. It is ours to show them in the salvation of our Lord Jesus Christ, and in personal communion with Him a joy unspeakable and full of glory that cannot be affected by any outside circumstances.

Some of us again will be called of God for foreign service to answer the challenge of the heathen millions. Perhaps we shall be called upon to undergo a test of the reality of our commission by weary months of waiting for outfit and passage money. But if truly called of God, this will only draw is closer to Him, lay a greater burden of prayer upon us, and send us out finally with greater determination than ever that we ourselves shall not be guilty of delay when the need is so great. We too must press forward, for it is no time for delay when a million souls a month pass into Christless graves in China, with other countries adding their hundreds of thousands. We must bring them that message that will deliver them from the power of Satan and bring them into the glorious liberty of the children of God.

For every Christian there is this challenge of man's need and of God's command to make all haste in the propagation of this gospel. Let us be sure that we are engaged in what is really His work, and then despite the difficulties, the remembrance of His faithfulness in the past will give us renewed hope and courage for the future.

People of God, does it not thrill our hearts today to realize that we do not answer such a challenge in our own strength? Think of it! God Himself is with us for our Captain; the Lord of Hosts is present in person in every field of conflict to encourage us and to fight for us. With such a Captain, who never lost a battle, or deserted a soldier in distress, or failed to get through the needed supplies, who would not accept the challenge to "Go forward, bearing precious seed."

John C. Stam

CHAPTER SEVEN

Journey to China

On September 24, 1932, with his missionary service on the horizon, John, along with five other single young men and a missionary couple with their child returning to the country, sailed for China third-class on the RMS *Empress of Japan.* They made stops along the way in Honolulu, Hawaii, and Yokohama, Japan.

John received a letter from Betty's father once he arrived in Japan, which made him believe he might have to fight for Betty's affection, as her outlook on not hearing anything from John continued to trouble her. Charles had visited John in person toward the end of June while he was at candidate training in Philadelphia. Dr. Scott rightly assumed John had written to his beloved daughter but that the letters were never obtained. He also understood the young missionary candidate's keen desire to someday marry Betty.

The *Empress of Japan* approached the coast of China on October 11. Since it was after ten in the evening when the ship finally docked along the Yangtze River in Shanghai, the decision was made to disembark the next morning. Stepping off the ship, John quickly saw the poor quality of life for so many. He had been prepared for the conditions beforehand from stories and photographs, but witnessing it firsthand deeply moved him. Less than forty-eight hours after being in Shanghai, he wrote home of those first impressions:

> I have seen people huddled together; men wearing next to nothing, and that pretty well in rags; faces that look full of suffering and sorrow; children with ugly-looking sores on their heads; miserable-looking eating places.

> May the Lord give us indeed to see a far deeper and far worse spiritual need: a soul that is starved and ready to pass out into eternity, an eternity of darkness; a life clad in rags instead of in the garments of righteousness; men that

71

are putrifying sores from head to foot in the sight of a living God. May the Lord show us their spiritual need, nor ever let us get so accustomed to poverty and suffering as to become insensible to another's need and no longer to have His heart of love that yearned over all men's troubles.

Since writing to John last, Betty had made a second trip to Shanghai to meet her parents when they arrived from America. Soon after, an infection of her tonsils forced Betty to make a third trip to the city. So unexpectedly, Betty happened to be there right as John was and the two managed to reconnect. Any doubts regarding how they felt about each other were quickly forfeited, as neither of them imagined such a chance meeting. Betty learned about the letter in which John proposed two months earlier but she never received. He explained his reasoning for waiting so long was to be sure he was acting in accordance with God's leading and not his own human desire. With sheer joy Betty accepted his proposal. John excitedly wrote in his diary on October 12:

> Hallelujah! Wonders never will cease. Our Heavenly Father so arranged it that Betty was here in Shanghai instead of being away up in northern Anhwei. She had to have tonsil tissue removed and was told to come on down for that. And she has promised to be my wife. How I do praise the Lord for all His ordering and arranging. He will not fail those who wait for Him.

Due to a rule the CIM had, engaged missionaries were required to wait a year before marrying. John wrote home about the impression the news made around him:

> And then everybody about the mission was so kind and so sympathetic too. You'd almost think they ought to have their doubts about a new missionary just coming out getting engaged right off the bat, but not a few of them noticed the coincidence of her being down here just at the right time.

John and Betty were able to spend six days together in Shanghai. During that period they went further into the city and purchased a simple wedding ring for Betty from a reputable jeweler. John desired to get a diamond ring for Betty, but she refused, seeing it as a hindrance to her work among the poor and feeling nobody else would be put off by her not having it.

On the morning of Tuesday, October 18, Betty left Shanghai to return to Fowyang (Fuyang today). Along with Mr. and Mrs. Glittenberg, recent appointees to the same city in the northwestern Anhwei Province, she would travel by train and then bus. By fall 1932, the work in Fowyang was carried out by three missionaries: a Presbyterian couple, E. H. and Estelle Hamilton, as well as a young woman, Nancy Rodgers, who worked with the girls' school. The Hamiltons were to go on furlough, and since the Glittenbergs had served elsewhere in China, they were appointed to take their place. Fowyang's three established missionaries gladly welcomed the much-needed support from the Glittenbergs and Betty. Katie Dodd, another single missionary who graduated from Moody and attended candidate school with Betty, also joined them.

The evening of that same Tuesday Betty left, John and a few other young men boarded a steamer to make a three-day trip up the Yangtze to Anking (Anqing today), in southeastern Anhwei, where they would spend several months in language school. He would not see Betty for another full year.

Twenty-three unmarried men from eight countries attended the school, which got underway on Monday, October 24. A routine schedule was followed Monday through Friday:

6:00 a.m.	Rising bell
7:30	Breakfast
8:00–8:20	English prayers
8:30–9:00	Chinese prayers
9:00–12:00	Classes and study
12:30 p.m.	Dinner
1:45–4:00	Classes and study
4:00–5:30	Exercise
5:30	Supper
6:00–6:20	Prayer for the provinces, CIM prayer meeting
7:00–8:00	Study
10:00	Lights out

The weekends at the language school did allow for some relaxation. They had Saturday afternoons free, and each week in the evenings a different student shared his personal testimony. Sundays were then devoted to worship. The students attended a Chinese service in the morning and an English one in the evening. John often used his time on weekends to catch up on his many correspondences with relatives and friends. The mission compound that became home for John was over a hundred square yards, and surrounded by high stone walls. Within these premises was a church building, separate missionary and native living quarters, a school, and an athletic field. Due to anti-foreign sentiment among some in Anking, students did not have the freedom to walk through the city whenever they wanted.

After gaining permission and venturing outside the compound, John became accustomed to many of the native cultural norms, such as foot binding on woman, a tendency toward valuing men over women, and ancestral worship. He also observed how small children tirelessly labored in the fields for their families. In one of his early weeks in Anking he overheard gunshots outside the city walls as military soldiers executed a number of communist rebels by firing squad.

The fall of 1932 for Betty was not without its hardships. She was grateful to be able to do hands-on work with the native people for the time being. Though Betty still had language study to complete, her already extensive knowledge of the Chinese language allowed her the opportunity to thoroughly minister in the region. Only a couple of weeks after arriving there, she went on a short itineration with Katie Dodd and a Chinese native, Miss Liu. The three headed in a southeastern direction from Fowyang and planned to evangelize among the local towns.

In a letter to her brother Kenneth, Betty wrote of experiencing the dry, desolate landscape along the way:

> Anhwei is the flattest country you ever saw in your life. It's almost like the ocean when very calm, with only here and there a bunch of trees and houses which can't be seen far off, as the houses are mud and the trees dusty, like everything else. Sometimes, the first we saw of a homestead was the bunch

of brilliant red peppers, hanging up to dry against a wall. These and the persimmon trees, which have a glorious way of turning color so that every leaf is a different hue, ranging from all oranges and reds to green, were almost the only bits of live color that we saw all day. Everywhere the people were harvesting pinky grey sweet potatoes, out of what looked like piles of dry dust. Whenever a little donkey trotted by, it raised a cloud of dust that could be seen for miles. Sometimes we were beside the river, which was almost blue, and had cut deep banks for itself out of dry cliffs.

Betty, Katie, and Liu traveled to multiple locations. Liu did most of the gospel sharing in the Chinese language as Betty and Katie distributed Christian tracts. Katie became sick toward the end of their journey and as a result headed back early to Fowyang that November.

Shortly upon their return, the group faced a devastating circumstance within the missionaries' circle. The youngest of the Glittenberg children, Lois, a lovely baby with golden curls, fell ill with dysentery. Mrs. Glittenberg headed to the closest hospital in Hwaiyuan (Haiyuan today), a long day's journey by bus. Along the way, the bus was stopped by rebel soldiers and the passengers were forced to get off. The soldiers went from passenger to passenger, taking what they had on them. One noticed the foreigner clinging to her small handbag and baby. Mrs. Glittenberg pleaded for the small bag, which contained the baby's medicine bottle and a few other personal items, but the soldiers were unconcerned. A soldier opened the bottle and the strong scent of alcohol quickly filled the air. Three soldiers proceeded to drink the entire bottle between them. The group of rebels then boarded the bus and drove away, leaving the passengers stranded. A long delay occurred before rickshaws could be found to take the travelers on their way. As a precaution, Mrs. Glittenberg had sewn money on the inside of her clothing so the soldiers couldn't find it and was able to pay her way into town, but long exposure ultimately cost the baby Lois her life. She died of dysentery at the hospital in Hwaiyuan. The loss was hard, but the couple's unshaken faith fortified them to remain in a land where God called them to serve. This deeply resonated with Betty, who wrote her outlook a few days after hearing the tragedy:

Here in this work, you just have to trust everything to God, including your children, and know that He will do exactly what is best, according to His will.

One major blessing for Betty that fall in Fowyang was the annual autumn conference. The conference was considered a tremendous success, with over eight hundred people in attendance, many coming in from outside districts. Eighty-two accepted Christ and were baptized during the occasion.

John and Betty were constantly in the other's thoughts as they wrote each week. Though some were delayed by the faulty mail service, the engaged couple's letters spoke of praises and troubles revealed in their respective areas as the year was coming to a close.

On Christmas Eve 1932, John wrote home telling his family about his own recent work and quoted a letter he got earlier from Betty regarding some of the difficulties she faced. At the end of the letter to Paterson, he proceeded to share a poem he had just received from Charles Scott.

The poem, titled "Afraid? Of What?" was written by missionary E. H. Hamilton after the martyrdom of one of his colleagues, Jack Vinson, at the hands of rebel soldiers in northern China. After Vinson was killed on November 2, 1931, a little Chinese girl who escaped relayed the information that became the inspiration for Hamilton's poem. The bandits had captured Vinson along with roughly three hundred Chinese. Recently recovering from an appendectomy, Vinson could not keep up with the other prisoners, and a soldier harshly poked him with a gun, asking if he was afraid. "No," he replied. "If you shoot, I go straight to heaven." When missionary friends found Vinson's desecrated body, they saw a bullet hole through his back, and upon wrapping the body in grass matting for preservation, his head rolled off.

Afraid? Of What?

Afraid? Of What?
To feel the spirit's glad release?
To pass from pain to perfect peace,
The strife and strain of life to cease?
Afraid—of that?

Afraid? Of What?
Afraid to see the Savior's face
To hear His welcome, and to trace
The glory gleam from wounds of grace?
    Afraid—of that?

Afraid? Of What?
A flash, a crash, a pierced heart;
Darkness, a light, O Heaven's art!
A wound of His a counterpart!
    Afraid—of that?

Afraid? Of What?
To do by death what life could not—
Baptize with blood a stony plot,
Till souls shall blossom from the spot?
    Afraid—of that?

John added before concluding his letter:

And so we can praise God that for us everything is well. If we should go on before, it is only the quicker to enjoy the bliss of the Savior's presence, the sooner to be released from the fight against sin and Satan. Meanwhile, we can continue to praise Him from whom all blessings flow.

CHAPTER EIGHT

Consecrated Couple

The school in Anking occupied most of John's time his first year in the country. Besides looking forward to marrying Betty in 1933, his other responsibility was to gain a strong sense of the Chinese language and culture. The weather turned cold during the winter season, and snow soon covered many parts of the country. John and Betty, in their separate cities, managed not to get sick due to the changing season.

On the evening of his twenty-fifth birthday, January 17, John noted in his diary:

> Today one quarter of a century of my life comes to an end. Tonight I have been much mindful of many failures and many opportunities missed. But I do thank God for those countless blessings all along the way, and look for His leading in the future. I give myself to Thee, Lord Jesus. Use me as Thy tool for Thy glory. Amen.

Two missionaries that John became fond of were Otis and Julia Whipple, an older American couple in Anking who would often alternate leading the Sunday English worship services on the organ. John greatly appreciated the musical ability they shared as it brought back childhood memories of his own family playing all their instruments in unison.

By early March, John was required to take the first language exam, a three-part endeavor that lasted as many days. A couple weeks later he had an oral exam and led a morning service in Chinese. John faced an extreme amount of pressure, but in the end came through. In his weekly letter to relatives, he wrote on March 25:

Hallelujah! Phew, that's been safely accomplished. I mean the Chinese prayers I took this morning. When we first began to study, and read what Hudson Taylor said about men preaching in Chinese six months after beginning to study, we smiled, but here it is just one day more than five months after I began to study, and I've already taken morning prayers. Praise the Lord.

I suppose it is because I've shaken in my boots so many times on different street corners all over Paterson that I'm not affected too badly that way these days, although I will admit that when I gave the class speech back in the Institute, I wasn't in an altogether cool state of mind, but this morning when I got up and faced my audience it wasn't too bad although one did wonder at the beginning if the mind would function as usual and call to mind that oh-so-small stock of words which make up my present Chinese vocabulary.

Nevertheless, it was with great thanksgiving to the Lord that I took on the job, and that I finished it, for it was certainly blessed to realize that I could say a bit, and get over some ideas which were apparently understood. Not being able to pray in Chinese yet myself, I asked the Chinese pastor to do so, and by the way he went over all the points of the message in his prayer it was evident that he had understood, even if he was repeating it all for the benefit of some others who may not have understood.

Dixon Hoste, CIM's general director, arrived at the language school two days later on Monday, March 27, for the purpose of interviewing the young missionaries and designating where they were to begin service in China. Hoste originally sailed to China in February 1885 as one of the Cambridge Seven, establishing recognizable prominence to CIM through their willingness to serve. He now acted as the Mission's second director since 1902, fulfilling the role after Hudson Taylor's resignation. The interviews Hoste conducted started that Monday after the students' morning devotions, but John's time with him came the following afternoon. The elderly director had a cold and had to conduct the interview from bed.

John said of the interaction: "There wasn't a suggestion of the army about him, and he seemed much more like a tired old patriarch, who has wanted for long to lay his burden down. The Mission is still praying about his successor, but it isn't clear yet who he is to be. As he sat there, the first thing that came into my mind was the picture we get in Genesis of the Patriarch Jacob leaning upon the top of his staff and blessing his sons."

John was in the room for only a few minutes when Hoste began to pray. For the next fifteen or twenty minutes, Hoste asked the Lord to bless John and Betty, the CIM, native church, and other missionaries. After praying, he spent the next hour humbly giving advice to John.

Referencing Hoste's 1929 appeal for two hundred new workers to carry the work in China, John said of his given assignment, "It is intended that we should open Tsingteh, a new station in the southwest. So, if I'm not out with the two hundred, it looks as if I shall go into the forward movement work after all. Praise the Lord."

John was first to go to Suancheng (Xuancheng today), a city about a hundred miles northeast of Anking. He would undertake further language study while serving with George and Grace Birch, a Canadian missionary couple from Vancouver, British Columbia, who came to China in 1928. The plan after getting married was for John and Betty to eventually establish the new mission in Tsingteh, roughly sixty miles south of Suancheng. Shortly after Hoste's visit, the students started leaving the language school for their new places of service.

On April 13, John left Anking to spend a month in Wuhu, where alongside Otis Whipple he helped in local secretarial work. John was then transported by boat on May 12 along the small river that ran from Wuhu to Suancheng. There he met George Birch, who later recalled their first meeting:

> How clearly I remember the day John arrived in Suancheng. I met him at the launch. He was six foot two, every inch a man. His hearty grip and bright smile clinched our friendship at once. As we proceeded in the sampan (little boat, for shallow water) the conversation soon turned to the things of God, for John lived with God and loved to talk of the things which were filling his heart.

The CIM's large compound established in Suancheng was a warm welcome. A vibrant children's ministry was underway at the mission, and it was planned for John to work with a young Chinese Christian, Mr. Ho, in overseeing this ministry. "It would be hard enough to hold the attention of such a rowdy lot of youngsters at home with a knowledge of my own language," wrote John after being settled for three days. "But if I am to have anything do with these little folk, it's not going to be any easier. So do pray for that."

Less than a week after their introduction, George Birch and John left for a ten-day itineration of towns and small villages between Suancheng and Kwangteh, a city sixty miles to the east. The excursion consisted mostly of preaching and handing out gospel tracts. Besides the men discussing both publicly and more intimately with those around them, George also hung up hymns and picture scrolls on buildings. Through this, thousands were receptive to the gospel message by word or print before the two came back on May 27. George reflected his sentiments:

> On our first itineration together we had to walk all one day in the rain and mud, but John's ardor was in no way dampened. That trip, and our trips together, were a blessing to me, for John's mind was a mine of wealth in the knowledge of God. He truly was mighty in the Scriptures, full of zeal to make Christ known, and full of love to the lost souls around him.
>
> John was very quick to see the hand of God in everything. He often used to say, "My heavenly Father knows." And once when speaking of difficulties to face he quoted the Lord's words, "For this cause came I unto this hour."

John reported positively on the journey two days after returning: "This is the type of work I hope to be doing for the years to come—getting out into the country, helping to build up the few struggling saints here and there, and preaching to the heathen in the towns and villages about, and in every tea shop along the road."

That spring and summer, Betty was also encouraged in her ministry endeavors at Fowyang. The Glittenbergs were transferred to a new station CIM opened in Kuoyang, a good distance north of Fowyang. A young seminary-trained native Christian, Miss P'eng, had come to work with Katie Dodd and Betty in the recent months. It was eventually decided that Miss P'eng and Katie would accompany the Glittenbergs when they eventually moved to Kuoyang, and minister to the women.

On June 28, George and Grace Birch left Suancheng for a two-month break at a quiet mountain resort. Chinese missionaries were typically able to spend a few weeks during the hottest parts of the summer at a cooler seaside or mountain resort. John had been invited to the Scotts' home in Tsinan but decided to stay in Suancheng. He wanted to further immerse himself in the language and help the local ministries. As the only male, he was now left with four female missionaries, so he helped with the children's programs for the remainder of that summer. He also helped cook and looked after the Birches' garden while they were away. The children were a great joy to John. Even though he could only understand a fraction of the language, John made use of Scripture and started putting Chinese words to music. Toward the middle of August he solemnly wrote:

> If dirty grass huts, and filthy naked children, and ulcers, sores, people minus noses, and with all kinds of physical troubles are grieving, and anything but good to look at, yet there's another side to it too. In one's own heart there can be peace that passeth understanding, and joy that will out. And about on the outside, one's own heart can be gladdened by hearing the children going down the street singing away at the top of their lungs, "Yes, Jesus loves me.'" I have been keeping up the children's meetings three times a week, and have been more than repaid in hearing the children sing their choruses just about all day long, so that if I cannot give the message to their folk, they most certainly do in the words of many scripture choruses.

By fall John had already made plans to meet Betty at her parents' residence in Tsinan for their October wedding. The honeymoon would be held in the bride's childhood home of Tsingtao. The first two weeks of October John worked vigorously at his studies in order to take the second major exam before leaving. "Was much helped of the Lord in learning some 280 characters in the writing lessons very quickly," he recorded in his diary on Wednesday, October 11. For the next two days he took his oral exam and three-part written test. That Friday evening John moved his belongings out of the house where he had been staying with the Birches and into the neighboring home that he and Betty would share when returning from their honeymoon. The next morning, John caught a ship from Suancheng to Wuhu.

Desiring to take a couple days off before leaving to meet Betty, John wrote a short letter of gratitude, sharing reasons for thanking and praising the Lord for his current situation:

1. That I'm saved and in the Lord's service.

2. For excellent health despite the hottest summer here in years and a change in climate too.

3. Great advance in the language.

4. Maybe this ought to be #2. That D.V. (Latin for "God willing") I shall soon be returning with "my wife"—I like that phrase too.

John got to Tsinan in the early morning of October 18 and eagerly made his way to the Scotts' home, where he met Betty exactly one year to the day when they parted in Shanghai. The couple enjoyed two days together at the Scotts' home before members of the wedding party arrived.

Betty chose Katie Dodd and Nancy Rodgers, her colleagues from Fowyang, as bridesmaids. Betty's maid of honor was her close friend Marguerite Luce, a roommate for three years from Wilson College and now a missionary nurse working in the Presbyterian hospital in Chefoo, China. For groomsman John picked Percy Bromley, who he had come to know during their time spent together at the language school in Anking. The wedding was officiated by the Scotts' neighbor, Rev. Reuben A. Torrey Jr., son of world-renowned American evangelist R. A. Torrey.

The weather on Wednesday, October 25, 1933, made for a perfect wedding scene. Not a cloud in the sky or winds to stir up dust. Around two hundred guests were invited, including many of the Chinese children taught by Betty's parents. The tennis court on the missionary compound was converted into an open-air chapel. Extended benches with backs were carried from the nearby church and arranged in a decorative semicircle with a wide aisle down the middle. All of this created a memorable backdrop for the many friends who witnessed the celebration.

Charles and Clara Scott reported to their supporters back home: "Everyone seemed to feel a reverence and sacred joy as they witnessed the uniting in holy wedlock of two such devoted, consecrated young lives. Many of the guests, Chinese and foreign, spoke later of the helpfulness of the service to them."

John wrote to his family afterward: "Despite our fears, the wedding went off beautifully, or at least so everybody said. About the only thing I know was that Betty looked very, very beautiful as she came down the aisle at her father's side. Then I led her to the minister and the words of that beautiful marriage ceremony began. After the ceremony we just turned in our places and greeted the guests."

In the same letter, he added of their honeymoon setting and activities:

I wish I could describe Tsingtao to you. Look up the map of the place in the Encyclopedia. It is built on a big peninsula, or series of them, with many high mountains and lots of woods. The place in which we stay, called a "Pension," is on the side of a high hill overlooking the beach, the far peninsula and the sea beyond. It's just gorgeous, and Betty and I are daily enjoying our walks around the hills. The trees are just turning and the air has that delightful autumn tang to it, so that we are thoroughly enjoying ourselves. We've been out to meals a few times to some old friends of the Scotts here in Tsingtao, but most of the time we are out walking, or home reading, and just simply enjoying ourselves. Incidentally, I guess this is the first real vacation I've had with nothing to do, for years and years.

On Wednesday, November 8, they boarded a ship for Shanghai. Three days later the newlyweds had a few professional portraits taken by a local studio, the prints of which were soon after sent to family and friends. While in the city, the Stams attended church services and prayer meetings, as well as a few meals with missionary acquaintances. On November 20, a steamer took them to Suancheng. It was well after midnight by the time John and Betty slipped into bed. The two were very pleased to be in the place they would call their first home.

To John, from Betty

How can I sing, and how pour out my heart,
When we are half the earth miles apart?
There is a Reason; 'Tis our Father's plan
That draws us each to each, woman and man;
Yet tries in tender care our love to Him:
Shall one his work forget, with zeal now dim?
Never, Oh Lord! For we would still be true,
Finishing first what tasks we have to do.
It is our Savior and our God indeed
Who made our love, and Who our lives will lead.
I love you, Dearest, who have won my love;
So understanding, kind, and wise you prove.
I love you, Sweetheart—what a joy is this;
You gave me, in Goodbye, a lasting kiss.
I love you, Darling—Oh, that loving might
Deep in your heart enfold me, day and night.
I love you, Darling; like a baby wee
That must be sheltered close, I treasure thee.
I love you, Lover; gentle man and strong,
Your love has swept me, unafraid, along.
I love you, Peter-Rock, who are so true,
Firm and reliable, I trust in you.
Not above God, and not before His name,
I love thy dear name next, Beloved John.
And in His time, and as He wills it so,
We shall come closer than as yet we know.

CHAPTER NINE

Serving as One

John and Betty expected nothing to be more wonderful than their two-week honeymoon but were completely surprised when married life brought them ever more happiness in carrying out mission work together. For their first days together in Suancheng they unpacked their belongings and got their new home settled until it was to their satisfaction.

While the couple had their own living quarters on the mission compound, John and Betty shared their meals in a separate space with George and Grace Birch to save on extra housekeeping. They spent many quiet evenings by their fireside, as John kept his books on one end of a table and Betty patiently studied at the other. She was preparing for the last of her language examinations in the coming months. John and Betty also immediately started helping with the children's meetings held each week and on Sunday evenings.

"John is out with George over the weekend, his first trip since we came home—and next weekend he and I are planning to visit another outstation, where he is to lead his first Communion service in Chinese," Betty wrote passionately to John's parents in December. "That will be my first trip in this part of the country. The weather is not very cold yet, but damp; not quite raining, but leaking dampness, so to speak. We have had the tailor and his men busy for some days, and both of us are now fixed up with fur-lined garments and others. You ought to see John in his Chinese garments! He looks taller than usual. And watch him gather his arms up under the skirts in back, when he is going downstairs, for all the world like an old Chinese gentleman."

Shortly before the Chinese New Year, in February 1934, John and Betty took a longer trip to the southern Anhwei Province where they were to establish residence later that year when another missionary couple, Mr. and Mrs.

Sam Warren, left on furlough. It would be a twenty-four-day itineration of the region, covering some two hundred miles on foot and another thirty-five by boat. One of their early stops was Tsingteh, where they spent a week examining the conditions and efforts of their future home. The Warrens had lived in the city for about a year, and before that missionaries had only stayed there occasionally. A small number of professing believers were among them, as the majority of the inhabitants tended to practice ancestral worship instead of Christianity. John commented:

> Ancestor worship with the strong clan systems form our greatest barrier throughout the whole region. The people there are mostly old families who have lived there for ages and generations, and ancestral halls are the things that are most prominent. Idols are very few in these places, mostly these great halls with bank upon bank of ancestral tablets rising up toward the ceiling. In Tsingteh alone there are said to be thirteen ancestral halls for the Lu family.

> For centuries back many of these people have been of the gentry class, with ancestors and relatives as officials at court to supply the means of living. Now they live on the proceeds of the clan property which is divided once a year, and anyone refusing to join in their ceremonies, and following the Christian doctrines, stands the chance of having his income cut off, and besides that being deprived the use of the family name. A farmer of the clan may find his fields taken away, or his water supply cut off. So, it is only the power of God that can work against powers of coercion.

> As a town Tsingteh doesn't look very inviting. During the Taiping rebellion seventy years and more ago, the greater proportion of the population was slaughtered, and cities were buried and ruined. Today garden walls are made of great piles of bricks that formerly were houses, while all around one sees doorposts and pieces of wall to remind one of the former glory of a once-flourishing town.

> But Tsingteh is certainly located for our field, so while it may be a little bit of a third-rate town, it is still the center for the district and a place which in itself needs to hear the gospel.

Betty expressed her own sentiments on the city and residence there:

> We have enjoyed the scenery around here very much, only it looks like
> another case of "Every prospect pleases and only man is vile." The gospel has
> been preached around these parts for many years, but there are practically
> no real Christians to show for it. They live in more comparative comfort, eat
> better food, and are probably more self-satisfied. Many live in old houses full
> of spacious halls, wonderful old carved wooden beams, and shutters. Even in
> the inns coming down, we rarely encountered a single flea or allied pest—a
> thing unheard of in the north. There are some lovely old stone bridges over
> clear-flowing streams. The rice fields everywhere are most picturesque. So
> are the high grass-covered mountains and the blue misty peaks behind them.
>
> We don't know when the Warrens leave here, and when we take over the
> premises. So maybe John and I shall be away for the summer, with Daddy
> and Mother at the seashore, possibly in Korea or North China. But they
> say there is still much talk of Japanese activities in the North, and no telling
> what may happen. Anyway, we are in His hands.
>
> Do pray about the beginning of work here. We really have a fine street chapel
> at the front, and a comfortable place in the rear, made out of one of the
> Chinese houses. It used to be an opium den, and then a cloth shop in front
> and a private school behind. Our place is now screened and all fixed up.

The Stams enjoyed visiting with a Pastor Cheng of Changhwa (Changhua
today) in the Chekiang Province (Zhejiang today) on February 21. Cheng
maintained a church with a faithful congregation of eighteen believers.
Approximately thirty years earlier, Pastor Cheng's father, then a schoolteacher,
bought a copy of the Gospels and Acts from a colporteur. He read the Scripture
for hours on end until he became convinced this was the message from the
true God. When the street salesman passed through a second time, Mr. Cheng
inquired if there was more to this story, as he since found out he only had one
part. So eventually Mr. Cheng came into possession of the whole Bible and
became a witness to many. He was baptized later by CIM missionary George
Gibb in his respective station. Shortly after this commitment to Christ, the new
convert's eyesight began to fail, and for nearly a month was blind. His neighbors

said it was due to him not worshiping idols, but he stood firm. When his grand-mother died sometime later, the same thing was stated. Mr. Cheng insisted that it was due to natural causes because of her being sixty years old. Lastly, his son became violently ill and when relatives' appeals to the father were unavailing, they finally went to the son, asking if they could worship and please the idols on his behalf. But he, too, stood firm and publicly proclaimed that they worshiped the one true God. Threats soon came to both father and son about taking over their house and fields, but they continued to stand firm. The son recovered and went on to become pastor of the church in Changhwa, continuing to share that spiritual bond with his now-elderly father. This portrait of unwavering loyalty to their faith struck a chord in John's and Betty's hearts.

Another of the many towns the couple went to was Miaosheo (Miaoshou today), arriving on February 24. John and Betty stayed two nights in the out-skirts with a widow, Mrs. Wang, the first individual to become a Christian in the entire region. Mrs. Wang's son and his family lived with her. She pro-ceeded to share her story of coming to Christ with the Stams. Several years before, George Gibb and his wife, Margaret, were passing through the district and came to Miaosheo at nightfall, looking for a place to stay. Mrs. Gibb, tired from their traveling, was in a sedan chair when Mr. Gibb began preach-ing in the street. Mrs. Wang heard the message and, believing its importance, grabbed her husband to listen. Mr. Wang accepted this new doctrine, and the couple invited the Gibbs to stay at their home. Afterward, when asked if Mrs. Wang believed the gospel, she replied, "How can one help but believe when told of such love?"

Toward the beginning of March, as John and Betty arrived back in Suancheng, they came to the joyous realization that Betty was carrying a child. Due to her weakened heart, Betty had to be carried during a good portion of the itineration in a sedan chair. Betty wrote to her parents about their recent travels. Clara Scott responded with a worried letter that nothing short of a miracle could prevent Betty from having trouble with her pregnancy after such a rigorous journey over so many miles. Betty insisted, however, that she was likely in better health because of her physical travels. Toward the end of that spring, Betty did end up becoming more careful due to her pregnancy.

With the increasing heat it started becoming apparent she would have to be careful how she conducted herself in ministry that coming summer.

The Birches were in Wuhu at the time, where Grace had just given birth to their second child, John Alfred, on March 4. Their first son, David, had already adapted to the Stams' presence at age two, and he jubilantly referred to them as "Uncle John" and "Aunt Betty."

John made a few more excursions that spring alongside Sam Warren and other CIM workers, including native colleagues. He returned to Miaosheo in early May, this time without Betty, and stayed again with Mrs. Wang. An important meeting took place this trip as he worked with a Chinese evangelist named Lo Ke-chou. Employed by CIM, Pastor Lo carried out most of his evangelistic work around Kinghsien (Jingxian today), and it was intended he would move with his family to Miaosheo later in the year to assist the Stams in their regional ministry.

Reflecting on this recent visit, John wrote: "Mrs. Wang's home is one of the great big old mansions of that part of the country, now worth very little because during the T'ai P'ing Rebellion, eighty years ago, the majority of the population was destroyed. When I'm at Mrs. Wang's, I'm a real clover, for she keeps the place very clean and cooks excellent meals. She knows what the foreigner likes and what's good for him. She just hovers over you like the dear old grandmother she is."

Near the end of his letter, he added of the city's current state, saying, "Pray for the Wang family. They are the bright spot in the Miaosheo church. There are others there, but some of them are a blot to the name of the church. We had a very good time the ten days we were in Miaosheo, visiting in the homes of the church members, most of whom are scattered through the hills around, and going to nearby villages to preach, distribute tracts, and sell gospels. On rainy days we found Miaosheo itself to be the best place to stay. With little to do, the storekeepers were very ready to listen, and we trust the Lord blessed the testimony."

John, Pastor Lo, and Sam Warren visited Tsingteh together, and then three more towns east, before John headed back to his own station, rejoining Betty on May 18.

CHAPTER TEN

Helen Priscilla

About six weeks later, in July 1934, John and Betty temporarily moved to Wuhu. Their main purpose for going was so that John could take over the duties of CIM's local secretary, Nathan Walton. Nathan and his wife, Lois, alongside their young daughter, Barbara Ann, wanted to get away to nearby primitive mountains for a two-month break. Lois was the daughter of missionaries, Otis and Julia Whipple, whom John had gotten to know in Anking. The other reason for relocating was to be closer to the hospital when Betty gave birth.

The secretary job was not an ideal fit for John, as noted in letters back home. He wrote July 18, also referencing his business school days:

> I'm very glad now that I did take up bookkeeping in Drake's when there, but like it not better than ever. The local secretary's work here requires a lot of pen work, and I never did specially like juggling figures through cash, books, journals, and ledgers. I like handling men and things much better than pens and figures. However, the dear chap who holds this job down here for us all through the year certainly deserves our thanks. He's as truly a missionary keeping us supplied with money, eats, etc. as we are, and he won't lose his reward. He's a very obligating fellow, and spends much of his time running around on errands for us that make things much more endurable when you go inland.

He revealed similarly, concluding a letter on August 2:

> I'm glad I'm not designated for work in a place like this. The local secretary's work does take time—bookkeeping, meeting boats, buying supplies, etc. etc. and while the house is in a lovely location, it is too far away from the

town itself for purposes of the work (real spiritual). They've asked me to preach in church on Sunday, for which I am thankful.

Despite her advanced stage of pregnancy, Betty was able to complete the fourth and final set of language exams CIM required of its women missionaries later that month. At the time, John had still been studying in preparation for his third exam.

The couple felt blessed to have a Christian native named Mei Tsong-fuh agree to start working for them that summer as their household servant, arranged through the Mission. The plan was for her to move with the Stams to Tsingteh later that year. Mei had been hospitalized with an infection in both her eyes. One eye was able to be treated, but the other got so bad that it had to be taken out and replaced with a glass eye. After her release from the hospital, she began working for John and Betty, who ended up assisting her with some of the required medical bills.

Toward the end of the second to last week of August, Donald Barnhouse, pastor of Tenth Presbyterian Church in Philadelphia, along with his secretary, made their way to John and Betty's in Wuhu as they were visiting parts of China attending regional conferences. They arrived in the early part of the day and spent the night at their residence. John had known Barnhouse as a teenager and for months eagerly awaited his visit.

On Thursday, September 6, Betty entered the hospital at the doctor's suggestion. Two days later, John informed family members:

> Incidentally, they want her to stay there for three weeks after to give her heart a good rest before getting around again. The doctor is a bit careful about that heart, which is another call for all our earnest prayers.

> However, she is very comfortable up there. The hospital is on a high bluff above the river, and from the porch outside her room she can look way up and down the river. Really it is a most ideal spot for a hospital, and we are thankful to have such a place here. I go up to see her twice a day on my bike. The Waltons are back tomorrow, which will relieve me of all responsibility for the house and the secretarial work.

The following Tuesday, September 11, 1934, Betty gave birth to a healthy baby girl at 3:15 in the afternoon. A caesarean operation was performed. Weighing six pounds, eleven ounces, the child was named Helen Priscilla Stam. Helen's first name was given after Betty's sister, while the middle name kept in line with her distinct ancestral heritage of the Aldens'.

Betty would not receive the doctor's clearance to be released from the hospital until nearly a month later—October 8. Two weeks after, Betty wrote a letter to John's parents informing them about their newest grandchild:

> The baby looks like John, nearly everybody says at first sight. She has his mouth and rather pointed chin. Her eyes are a deep blue, and very big, and her face is so sweet and round, with a lot of dark hair (that may be turning lighter, we aren't sure), that is actually curly when damp . . .

> It is a real joy to take care of her. We can't say she never cries; in fact, she usually spends several hours of the daytime awake and howling; but even then, she takes little naps at intervals, besides good long naps too, and during the night she sleeps soundly from 10 p.m. to 6 a.m., and most of the time from 6 to 10 p.m. too.

She added this about being a young mother left in charge:

> I am always wondering if she is too warm or too cold, and rushing around to feel her hands and feet. She won't keep her arms inside the bedclothes, so I pile on an extra knitted jacket, backside front. Last evening she howled and kicked so hard that she put her feet right through a little flannelette gown that Mother Scott had made for her, only washed a few times: I'm afraid it was temper; for the minute anybody picks her up, she is as placid and serene as she can be, with a slightly reproachful expression, as much as to say, "Why didn't you come sooner?" So we shall have to be very strict with her.

Clara Scott traveled from Tsinan to aid Betty with Helen for two weeks. They were excited to share Betty's newlywed sister, Beatrice, for three days, who, along with her husband, Theodore Stevenson, arrived shortly before in China to begin their missionary service under the Presbyterian Board, USA. Theodore was son of Princeton Theological Seminary's then president, J. Ross Stevenson.

On Friday, October 19, John set out once again for southern Anhwei. This time he was accompanied by CIM missionary Erwin Kohfield who was stationed in Tunki (Tunxi today), approximately thirty miles south of Tsingteh. Kohfield's station was the closest to where John and Betty would be settling. Erwin and his wife, Mary, along with their three children, were forced to flee Tunki in late September when communist soldiers invaded. The family was able to escape and hid on a nearby mountain. Afterward, CIM officials quickly brought the Kohfields back to Suancheng where they had stayed the past three weeks.

Erwin Kohfield was eager to get back to Tunki just as John was to occupy Tsingteh, but William Hanna, the CIM Superintendent in Anhwei, requested they both find out if it was safe to do so. John was not only cautious of his movements, but also prayerful. Now that he had a wife and child to think of as well as work, he did not take the potential dangers lightly.

On October 25, in Tsingteh, John and Erwin met with the district magistrate, Mr. Peng. When John inquired about the conditions of the area, the conversation went back and forth regarding a small group of bandits in the region. John remarked of not wanting to risk meeting up with communists, to which Mr. Peng emphatically answered, "Oh, no, no! There is no danger of communists here. As far as that is concerned, you may come at once and bring your family. I will guarantee your safety, and if there should be any trouble you can come to my yamen."

After further investigating with the magistrate at Tunki on October 27, the two missionaries received the same assurance of protection. Based on the word from these two administrators, the Stams and Kohfields were given permission by CIM officials in Wuhu to proceed with their families to southern Anhwei.

From Wuhu, John and Betty spent several days in Suancheng with the Birches helping run a short-term Bible school before packing up and saying goodbye to the many friends they had come to appreciate during their year of residence.

Their final Sunday in Suancheng, November 18, a child dedication took place during the Chinese service. John and Betty dedicated Helen to the Lord, as did the Birches with their infant son, John. The officiating minister,

Rev. H. A. Weller, a missionary from Anking, was handed Helen by John. She was prayed over wearing a pink bonnet.

"It was very impressive and very blessed," John wrote of the service to family members the next day. "Both babies behaved wonderfully, our little Helen quite enjoying herself when she was awake, doing nothing. Mr. Weller prayed that she might be like Priscilla in the Bible, a help to the church, and minister to the saints. Incidentally we have transliterated Helen as nearly as possible into 'Ai-lien'—and at Mr. Weller's suggestion we took that particular 'Lien' that means a link or chain, so that her name in Chinese means a 'Love Link.' She surely is a darling, and behaves wonderfully. She has her crying spells, but those are valuable too. If I can find it, I shall enclose a recent photograph. More are coming."

CHAPTER ELEVEN

By Life or by Death

John and Betty had their household goods transported by hired servants on five wheelbarrows the sixty miles from Suancheng to Tsingteh. On November 22, 1934, the Stams set out for their new residence in southern Anhwei by bus with some of their personal luggage. Due to overcrowding on the public bus, they were put on one the military was using headed in the direction of Tsingteh. The chartered military bus, transporting two large guns and eight soldiers, took a mere three hours, as the bus was able to roll past the red flags that signaled public transportation to stop at small wayside stations. The next day, after the military bus reached the end of its line, the couple was blessed with beautiful weather as they walked across two high mountain passes and a valley into Tsingteh. The weather soon after turned rainy and considerably colder.

Two days later, on Sunday, November 25, they held their first church service. The service was attended by their household servants, one of the carriers they hired, a visitor from a nearby outstation, two outsiders who drifted in briefly, and a young girl. John, Betty, and their household servants were the only ones present at their service the first week of December. A few of the evenings, John was able to share with those around town as they wandered in from the street. By this point John had also arranged in late November through letters to their respective locations for Pastors Cheng and Lo to meet him in Miaosheo on December 7.

This news was shared with his relatives on December 5: "I have opened the street chapel some five times since being here nights, and have fairly attentive audiences. Do be praying for us." He added, "The people here seem quite friendly, and several men have been in with whom I have been able to have a good talk. God help us to open the Scriptures to them. This weekend I hope to go with Pastor Cheng to Miaosheo, and we hope to give out some famine relief funds which have been contributed for this district."

Though they had been assured of safety, John's suspicions of a communist presence were apparent in his last diary entry, written that ever-so-peaceful night: "Rumors are around about Reds east of Chiki—they say Chiki people have been losing sleep on account of the fear."

Using unfrequented paths, the Red Army's 19th division crossed the mountains behind government forces undetected. The city's own militia was no match against the Reds unit of two thousand soldiers when they attacked Tsingteh the next morning. The Reds killed three officials upon taking over the magistrate's headquarters. Viciously looting the town, they took people's food, money, and numerous other valuables. Fourteen of Tsingteh's headmen were killed, each the leader of a group belonging to ten families. Some of the wealthy citizens were killed while others were let go after their capture.

Arriving at the magistrate's prison, some of the prisoners were released to make room for the Stams. More than twenty other locals had also been taken captive and held for ransom. As gunshots rang aloud through the city, Helen Priscilla began to cry. Held in the comfort of her parents' arms, the soldiers guarding the Stams discussed whether they should kill the infant to save the army the trouble. An elderly male prisoner who was just released overheard and objected to the soldiers. Believed to be a simple farmer, the man argued that this innocent baby had done nothing worthy of death.

"Then it's your life for hers!" a soldier threatened, and the man replied, "I am willing." There on the spot he was hacked to pieces, and as a result, Helen was spared. Several reports afterward stated the man was a Christian, but there has never been proof for this claim as he was never identified. That evening John wrote his letter notifying CIM of their capture. There was no shadow of doubt in their faith, for John knew the possibility of what was ahead.

The next day at four in the morning, the Reds started taking the Stams twelve miles south toward Miaosheo. Traveling over the same mountainous roads they had walked before, John carried Helen on his back while Betty was able to ride a horse part of the way. The Stams' cook, Li Ming-chin, went to the prison to look for John and Betty but discovered they had already been moved. The Stams arrived in Miaosheo sometime later that day. While the

Army pillaged the town, they were temporarily forced into the postmaster's shop and left under guard.

"Where are you going?" asked the postmaster, recognizing the couple from passing through before. "We don't know where they are going," John simply replied, pointing to some of the soldiers. "But we are going to heaven." The postmaster offered some fruit to the couple and paper for John. Betty took the fruit, for she had Helen to nurse. John declined, instead taking time to write another letter to CIM officials in Shanghai. Even though John possessed no stamps, the postmaster later gave the letter to mission workers who had it forwarded to Shanghai.

> Miaosheo, Anhwei
> December 7, 1934
>
> China Inland Mission
>
> Dear Brethren,
>
> We are in the hands of the Communists here, being taken from Tsingteh when they passed through yesterday. I tried to persuade them to let my wife and baby go back to Tsingteh with a letter to you, but they wouldn't let her, and so we both made the trip to Miaosheo today, my wife traveling part of the way on a horse.
>
> They want $20,000 before they will free us, which we have told them we are sure will not be paid. Famine relief money and our personal money and effects are all in their hands.
>
> God give you wisdom in what you do and give us grace and fortitude. He is able.
>
> Yours in Him,
> John C. Stam

That night the Stams were taken to a local deserted house that once belonged to a wealthy man. Inside a room of the large home, John was tied standing to the bedpost. Betty was sufficiently restricted to prevent escape, but unbound, allowed to attend to her baby.

Around ten in the morning on Saturday, December 8, the communist soldiers decided to make an example of John and Betty to the local people. Both were tightly bound by rope, hands behind their back, and marched to the street. To add humiliation, the Stams had been stripped of their garments down to their wool underwear, with John wearing a white shirt and Betty wearing a man's blue shirt. John walked barefoot since he had given Betty his black socks to help protect her feet. Going through the streets, the soldiers ordered some of the surrounding townspeople to come witness the execution of these "foreign devils," reasoning they had ruined China and drained them of their resources.

Only one man, Chang Hsiu-sheng, spoke up on behalf of the couple. Chang, an elderly single man from the Hunan Province who worked as a medicine seller, specializing in dermatology, was a member of the local Miaosheo church. Although it is not confirmed how much of an established relationship John and Betty shared with Chang during one of their prior visits, the brave result was nothing short of intervention. Just days earlier, Chang was struggling with the ability to publicly express his faith. Taking a risk to help these foreigners, he pleaded on his knees in the street for the Stams' release. He offered to gather money from several residents, but to no avail, as the Reds only wanted American currency. One soldier told Chang that if somebody was able to hand over even a single American dollar, the couple would be let go. Disappointed at not being able to help, Chang went home. A soldier was sent to follow him and discovered a Bible and hymnal inside, leading to speculation that Chang was in league with the Stams. He was taken prisoner upon leaving Miaosheo later that night and killed at the next town the Reds invaded.

The soldiers were gentle with the villagers and handed out food stolen from the wealthy, along with propaganda pamphlets used to promote their causes. At the end of Miaosheo's main street, outside of town, stood Eagle

Hill. The growing crowd of peasants was told to proceed to Eagle Hill where there was a pile of clothing for them to take from, unaware of what they were about to witness.

John walked ahead as Betty followed closely behind. Shortly after reaching the hill, one of the soldiers jabbed his gun at John ordering him to kneel. Getting down on one knee, John spoke a few inaudible words to his captors, which the residents weren't close enough to hear. A young soldier believed to be in his late teens then stepped forward with a large sword and slashed John's throat. His lifeless figure went forward to the ground as his severed head, skin barely attached, fell beside. He continued speaking those final words until the execution. Still bound, Betty quivered, falling on both knees next to John. Glancing over one last time at her husband, knowing what was about to take place, Betty didn't scream or flinch. As she uttered a silent prayer, the same blood-stained sword cut through the back of Betty's neck, her body falling upon John's.

The soldiers returned to town, leaving the corpses where they lay among the pine trees of Eagle Hill. When the Reds dispersed, many of the spectators wept bitterly as they went back to their homes, knowing they had been used. Word of the young couple's death quickly spread through the region, as well as rumors of a baby left behind.

When news reached the mission's headquarters in Shanghai, many of the missionaries became fearful. Frank Houghton (1894–1972), editorial secretary for China Inland Mission at the time, decided to visit missionary outposts throughout China to check on those serving. While traveling over the mountains of Szechwan, the comforting words of 2 Corinthians 8:9—"though He was rich, yet for your sake He became poor"—were transformed into this now traditional Christmas hymn.

Thou Who Wast Rich Beyond All Splendor

1. Thou who wast rich be - yond all splen - dor, All for love's sake be -
2. Thou who art God be - yond all prais - ing, All for love's sake be -
3. Thou who art love be - yond all tell - ing, Sav - ior and King, we

cam - est poor; Thrones for a man - ger didst sur - ren - der,
cam - est man; Stoop - ing so low, but sin - ners rais - ing,
wor - ship Thee. Em - man - u - el, with - in us dwel - ling,

Sap - phire - paved courts for sta - ble floor. Thou who wast rich be -
Heav'n - ward by Thine e - ter - nal plan. Thou who art God be -
Make us what Thou wouldst have us be. Thou who art love be -

yond all splen - dor, All for love's sake be - cam - est poor.
yond all prais - ing, All for love's sake be - cam - est man.
yond all tell - ing, Sav - ior and King, we wor - ship Thee.

WORDS: Frank Houghton; MUSIC: *Quelle Est Cette Odeur Agreable* (French Carol).

CHAPTER TWELVE

The Miraculous Rescue

Unaware of the tragic developments in Tsingteh, Pastor Lo, along with his wife and four-year-old son, arrived in Miaosheo the evening of December 6 as planned in preparation to meet with John the day after. They spent the night at the home of Mrs. Wang and her family. In the morning a group of soldiers were seen entering the city. Not sure whether they were Nationalist or communist troops, the women and children in the house were sent to the foot of the mountain as a precaution. Mrs. Wang stayed behind as her son and Lo planned to investigate.

With the first appearance of soldiers, Lo and Mrs. Wang's son lingered around the main street to view what was happening. The lead officer of the Reds was seeking the headman of the town, and a soldier pointed out the two. Mrs. Wang's son ran for his life, for he was indeed a young leader in the community. Lo stood his ground and was taken captive by a Red officer. Lo was searched, losing money his father recently gave him. He was then briefly interrogated with questions about the town's militia before being asked to have someone identify him. Knowing a local friend was aware of his travels, he led the officer to the residence of Chang Hsiu-sheng, the same individual who would plead for John and Betty's life the next day. "This man is a stranger here," Chang truthfully stated. "I know him. He distributes tracts and treats diseases, as I do. He only came last night to Miaosheo." Not making the connection that the "tracts" were Christian publications or the "diseases" Lo treated was sin, the officer let him go. "It is all well," Chang concluded. Lo politely bowed and walked slowly to a back street before rejoining Wang's son, their wives, and children at the base of the mountain. The group all climbed the mountain and stayed the night there along with about a dozen others who had escaped that day. Not daring to make a fire for fear of being seen, the group suffered cold and hunger. Their only source of food was wild chestnuts. They had a single quilt to share between them, while one man in their party used a sickle to cut grass for covers as they slept.

Mrs. Wang remained at her home where a group of Red soldiers spent the night. She didn't know John and Betty were being held captive in town. While the soldiers didn't physically harm her, they took nearly her entire harvest of rice when they left the following day, and what they did not carry away they dumped in the pond outside her home. The money and few possessions left inside were stolen.

A rumor carried among other refugees had reached the small group in the mountain that a foreigner was being held captive by the Reds. Lo thought it might be the priest from Tsingteh's Roman Catholic church, as he hoped John, Betty, and Pastor Cheng were able to escape the city or postpone their meeting in time.

Even as the Stams were being led to their execution the next morning, the 78th brigade of Nationalist forces were in the vicinity of Miaosheo. Those in the mountain spotted them closing in from a distance. At about noon, the Nationalist troops opened fire on the Reds from a wooded ridge just outside town. A couple Reds were killed in the gunfire, but little retaliation was given. For several hours both parties were at a standstill, seeing who would make the bolder advance. The 19th Division withdrew from Miaosheo that night around ten, setting fire to houses along the road, and moved three miles to the next town where they rejoined the main Red Army Group, the 10th Division.

Earlier in the day a refugee reported back to Lo and his group on the mountain of a foreign couple killed. This news nearly confirmed the suspicions that the rumor had in fact been connected to John and Betty. They were able to start a fire to keep warm that second night. The next morning, Sunday, December 9, the party made their way down the mountain and back into town. Lo asked various townspeople about the location of the foreigners' bodies, but most were afraid to talk as they knew the Reds could return at any moment and spies were often known to be used throughout the region.

When he asked about his Christian friend, Chang, who had vouched for him two days before, Lo was told he spoke up for the couple the previous morning but that his current whereabouts were unknown. Lo finally learned that John's and Betty's bodies were on Eagle Hill. As he hurried down the street, an old woman approached and said that a foreign baby was left behind in one of the homes. Pointing out the specific building to him, he immediately went there. Upon entering, Lo passed several rooms which showed traces of the bandits' presence. After he heard a small cry from an inner room, he found baby Helen on the bed, bundled in the sleeping bag she was forced to be left in almost thirty hours earlier. Pinned inside the layers of clothes were two Chinese five-dollar bills her mother had tenderly hidden in hope that someone would discover Helen and use the money to provide for her needs. Also tucked away was a clean baby nightgown and some diapers, retrieved back home by her father the afternoon of their capture. The exact reason why Helen wasn't taken the morning of John and Betty's execution is unknown. Some suggest she was hidden by her parents or left by the soldiers to fend for herself. Others believe that due to the giving of a life for hers the Reds honored the sacrifice.

Carrying Helen with him, Lo made his way to Eagle Hill. Finding the grievous sight of the bodies that lay there was so much a shock that at first Lo could barely bring himself to look at the corpses. Returning to town, Lo left the infant in the care of his wife and went with Mrs. Wang's son to purchase a pair of coffins on credit, as well as four white sheets to wrap the bodies. Keeping with Chinese custom, lime was filled in for preservation.

Lo returned to Eagle Hill with Mrs. Wang, her son, and a few poor people who were hired to take care of the bodies. Birds flew above as stray dogs scoured the ground near the Stams, but Lo and his company arrived in time so that the bodies weren't desecrated. The peasants were paid to reattach the severed heads onto the torsos by sewing with hemp thread. Mrs. Wang later commented that John's face bore a smile, and Betty's was calm in repose. Besides bruise marks on their wrists from the bound rope there were no other signs of physical violation. After the bodies had been carefully wrapped and placed in the coffins, the three Christians knelt in prayer. A crowd gathered to watch and some of the local citizens expressed sorrow for what happened to the young couple. A few of the townspeople even cursed the communists for their hostile actions.

When Lo finished praying, he stood and addressed the crowd:

> You have seen these wounded bodies, and you pity these foreigners for their suffering and death. But you should know that they are children of God. Their spirits are unharmed and at this minute are in the presence of God. They came to China and to Miaosheo not for themselves but for you, to tell you about God and His love, that you might believe in the Lord Jesus Christ and be saved eternally. You have heard their message. Remember it is true—their death proves that. Do not forget what they told you—repent and believe the gospel.

Many of the listeners wept as Lo spoke. George Birch later commented on the unusual reaction:

> Personally I have not seen weeping in response to a gospel message in China. Why the change? Why the melted hearts? They had had a demonstration of the power of God, and the truth of the gospel. We expect much fruit from the glorious death and the faithful testimony of these two shining ones.

Persistent rumors of the communists returning to Miaosheo caused Lo to face a hard decision of what to do next. His young son was seriously ill from the two treacherous days in the mountains, but he also didn't want to risk putting Helen and his own family into more potential danger. After careful consideration, Lo and his wife set out north on foot for Kinghsien. The couple hired a pair of servants who took turns between them to carry baby Helen and their son in rice baskets at opposite ends of a bamboo plank. The infants slept but the little boy's condition appeared to be worsening. The next day, Lo was able to secure sedan chairs to transport his wife and him the remainder of the way to Kinghsien. To the relief of Lo and his wife, their boy's health had greatly improved. After several hours of semiconsciousness, he sat up in his basket and sang a hymn.

The Los found several young Chinese women who were willing to nurse Helen as they made their way to Kinghsien. Once they arrived, powdered milk was bought with the money left in the baby's clothing. From that, Mrs. Lo fed her on a regular three-hour schedule. Incredibly, the Los' child, like Helen, had also been born in the Methodist hospital in Wuhu, and Mrs. Lo still possessed the bottle from their son's birth to feed Helen. There was likely not another woman in all the district facing their circumstance who could have cared for her as Mrs. Lo did.

As Pastor Lo was seeking to get Helen back to missionary friends, telegrams began to spread in China to CIM officials in Shanghai regarding the disturbances in southern Anhwei, with the delayed news reaching them on the evening of Monday, December 10. Due to the fighting and poor lines of communication in China at the time, new and reliable reporting came at a slow rate. The uncertainty about the couple as well as Helen's whereabouts was widely broadcast in the media. The families of John and Betty, as well as believers in several countries, began fervently praying for their protection and release.

On Thursday, December 13, William Hanna received a letter from the Wuhu magistrate informing him that the Stam's bodies had been found in Miaosheo. The next day as lunch was being served, a knock came at George Birch's missionary residence in Suancheng. His wife and two boys were in Wuhu. Taking the moment in, George didn't realize at first the weary woman standing at his door was Mrs. Lo. Unable to control her tears, she extended a bundle to him and said brokenly, "This is all we have left." Assuming her husband had been killed by communists and this was her young son, George carefully loosened the cover, only finding to his amazement the beautiful sleeping face of Helen Priscilla Stam. Altogether, the Los and hired servants had made a nearly seventy-five-mile passage through bandit-infested mountains with their limited supplies over the four nights. Mr. Lo then came inside and gave an account of the past week's events as best he knew. The details surrounding the day of John and Betty's capture were later described by those who lived with them and locals in Tsingteh. It was also later found that Pastor Cheng, who was supposed to meet Lo and John on December 7, did manage to escape Miaosheo. Collectively it was decided to bring Helen to Wuhu by train where her condition could be checked at the Methodist hospital, as well as reunite with other missionary families. Laura Woosley, the region's provincial nurse and a graduate of the Bible Institute of Los Angeles, also made the additional twenty-five-mile trip.

Helen arrived in Wuhu later that evening around eight. The next day, December 15, she was brought to the hospital, where its superintendent, Dr. Robert Brown, along with staff, pronounced her to be in excellent health—without an upset stomach or even a cold. Charlotte Hsia, one of the Chinese nurses who helped deliver Helen at birth, fed her after the checkup. An American missionary by the name of Howard Smith, who had also recently come to Wuhu with his family, encountered the group as they arrived the previous night, and asked if he could take photographs of Helen, hoping to get them back to the American press. Howard, along with his wife and now two-year-old son, had previously been captured on May 8 by communist bandits. The wife and son were let go and told to obtain the equivalent of $30,000 for Howard's release. After fifty-two days of hardship in the mountain where he was being held with other prisoners, Howard and a Chinese boy made an escape. When the Smith family was reunited, they would be transferred to the Anhwei Province, but coincidentally fled their town the night of December 8 after hearing of the attack on nearby Tsingteh. At the time, Howard was still a large target for the communists as a result of his disappearance that summer.

Howard Smith made a series of photos with Helen, both on the way to the hospital and afterward of those who helped in her aid. The photos would soon be relayed to America, and many were published through media outlets the following month. One in particular, as wide eyes looked out just past the camera, became the most famous picture symbolizing the Stams' story.

"After Helen's rescue, missionaries stationed in Wuhu were all eager to have their picture taken with her," recalls Ray Smith, Howard's son. "As some of my dad's photos would later be widely seen both in newspapers around the world and in Christian publications, our family was disappointed dad was always behind the lens and never got either himself or our mom, Gertrude, pictured with Priscilla. We can be thankful, however, that he was at just the right place and time to capture those poignant images."

The missionaries were careful of not making Helen's presence known during the next two weeks for fear of possible retaliation from the Reds.

William Hanna and Laura Woosley proceeded to take a dedicated two-day journey with Helen, one by boat and then train to Tsinan, where she was put into the secure care of her maternal grandparents on December 28.

Shortly after Helen's arrival to Wuhu, Lois Walton wrote to Charles and Clara Scott:

> I am so anxious for you to see little Helen, for she is simply perfect! She is a beautiful baby, so well and strong and as good as gold. She scarcely ever cries. And she is such a dear combination of Betty and John. Her eyes are just like Betty's. She smiles most of her waking moments, and coos and talks so sweetly!

By the time Chiang Kai-shek was notified of the Stams' death, the news had already reached the general population, which in turn troubled foreign relations between the United States and China. After Nationalist troops recovered Tsingteh on December 14, at another town within the Anhwei Province, more than four hundred communist bandits were killed and over one hundred others captured. Severely questioned one by one, four of the captured men confessed to their involvement of murdering Americans in Miaosheo. Upon being court-martialed in Tunki, the four were executed on the spot by simultaneous beheading on December 22 as retribution. By the end of January, the entire 10th Red Army Group was wiped out by Nationalist forces.

Multiple lives were gone, others risked their own, all as this infant who couldn't comprehend what transpired was provided the chance to thrive. In light of the miraculous series of events in Helen Priscilla's survival and deliverance to safety, she was dubbed, first by those in China, and then Christians around the world, "the Miracle Baby." Like Moses of the Old Testament when discovered along the Nile River, the precious child was three months old. She would begin to take the world in her arms, and the world soon took her into theirs.

Within the last week of December 1934, the Stams' maid and cook started going through their deserted home in Tsingteh, retrieving personal effects, and working with CIM officials to get possessions back to the respective families. On a piece of trampled paper used to wrap dishes were the following lines, penned by Betty six years prior while studying at Moody. The bottom was signed with her girlhood name, Elisabeth A. Scott.

Open My Eyes

Open my eyes, that I may see
This one and that one needing Thee,
Hearts that are dumb, unsatisfied,
Lives that are dead, for whom Christ died.

Open my eyes in sympathy.
Clear into man's deep soul to see;
Wise with Thy wisdom to discern,
And with Thy heart of love to yearn.

Open my eyes in power, I pray,
Give me the strength to speak today,
Someone to bring, dear Lord, to Thee,
Use me, O Lord, use even me!

CHAPTER THIRTEEN

Global Impact

When confirmation of John and Betty's deaths reached the United States the morning of December 13, a reporter found Cornelius Stam alone at the Star of Hope Mission and broke the news. Shaken by the account, he immediately called his brother Jacob and together went to tell their mother at home. Amelia Stam was outside wearing a large apron when Neil and Jacob told of the tragedy. After the realization settled in, she went over to sit underneath the set of outdoor front stairs, and with the apron pulled up over her face, openly wept. The brothers read Psalm 46 in an attempt to comfort her. Acting as spokesperson for the Stam family, Cornelius told the local paper: "We know that while they are absent from the body, they are present with the Lord. Their confidence was in the Lord and our confidence is in the Lord and that confidence is not misplaced whether they serve Him on earth or there in Heaven." *The Paterson Evening News* front page from that day printed a bold headline:

JOHN STAM AND WIFE SLAIN BY CHINESE;
U.S. DEMANDS ACTION
Bodies Of Paterson Missionaries Found In Ditch;
Baby Still Missing; Family Here Stunned By News

Peter Stam, who was away in New York on business, soon received word through a telegram from CIM expressing their condolences. Just days prior on December 10th, he got a letter from John about his family moving into new territory and once again included the "Afraid? Of What?" poem. Peter wrote, conveying the news to friends and supporters:

Our dear children, Mr. and Mrs. John C. Stam, have gone to be with the Lord. They loved Him, they served Him, and now they are with Him. What could be more glorious? It is true, the manner in which they were sent out of this world was a shock to us all, but whatever of suffering they may have endured is now past, and they are both infinitely blessed with the joys of Heaven.

As for those of us who have been left behind, we were once more reminded of our sacred vows by a telegram received from one of John's schoolmates in the Midwest—"Remember, you gave John to God, not to China." Our hearts, though bowed for a little while with sadness, answered, "Amen!" It was our desire that he, as well as we, should serve the Lord, and if that could be better done by death than by life, we would have it so. The sacrifice may seem great now, but no sacrifice is too great to make for Him who gave Himself for us.

We want to express our deepest gratitude to the many friends in Christ who have leaped to our support in this hour of trouble. Some may be wondering if our faith has been shaken. Praise God, it has not. Indeed, it has been greatly strengthened by the many portions of the Word of God which have been sent to encourage us. They poured in by letter and by telegram and by telephone. We thank God too, for the dear Christian friends who came to us in our grief and clasped our hands and whispered verses of Scripture into our ears.

After the news of the slaying of Betty and John had been published, we still received a number of letters telling us that a great volume of prayer was going up for their release from their Communist captors. These many friends need not feel that their prayers were unanswered. They were answered, for Betty and John were released . . . They were released from the pain and toil of life, and brought gently into the presence of the Savior whom they loved so dearly.

We are earnestly praying that it will all be for God's glory and the salvation of souls. How glad we shall be if through this dreadful experience many souls shall be won for the Lord Jesus! How glad we shall be if many dear Christian young people shall be inspired to give themselves to the Lord as never before, for a life of sacrifice and service.

We were honored by having sons and daughters minister for our Lord among the heathen, but we are more signally honored that two of them have received the martyr's crown.

We are sure that our dear brother and sister, Dr. and Mrs. C. E. Scott, both join us in saying, "The Lord gave and the Lord hath taken away; blessed be the name of the Lord." (Job 1:21)

What made John and Betty's story unique for its time was that news of their martyrdom was spread so far throughout the world. Christian missionaries' deaths up to this point in history had never been publicized in newspapers and on the radio like the Stams' were. Given the circumstances during their last days, hundreds of newspapers covered the unfolding events weeks after, many of which ran headlines and articles across the front page. At least one paper from each US state published an article on their deaths and Helen's remarkable rescue. Major outlets such as *The New York Times*, *Chicago Tribune*, *Time* magazine, and the *Associated Press* all contributed to spreading their testimony, providing a thorough witness to those who came across the articles. A national interest in political affairs with China was also rekindled through this reporting.

The following days after the news broke, the Stams had hundreds of friends come to them with words of condolences. The family felt the most sympathy though for those who didn't reach out because they couldn't make sense of what happened.

"Oh, why did they go there!" a lady in Paterson said with grief. "Because the love of Christ constrained them," Peter replied. "They loved the Lord and the Chinese people—that's why they went to China. We were glad to see them go, and would gladly have them go again, because we look not at the things which are seen. They were not after money or comfort, but after souls."

Among the most touching condolences received by Mr. and Mrs. Stam was from one of the sons of Jack Vinson, whose death in China inspired the poem that had become a favorite to John and Betty.

As my father was captured and killed by bandits three years ago in North China, I feel that I may offer you my sympathy. But what a blessed privilege is ours in having our own dear ones go the limit in service for the Master! To me, this joy has taken the place of sorrow.

On the other side of the world, news of their death came to the Scott parents in China the evening of December 13. The fate of Helen Priscilla was still unknown at this time but was assumed she wouldn't have survived the turmoil that ensued. When Charles and Clara first discovered the series of events, they sent for R. A. Torrey Jr. to come over as soon as possible. Dr. Scott told Torrey all he knew, and both proceeded to go upstairs to visit Mrs. Scott. Dr. Scott and Dr. Torrey prayed, both breaking down while trying to make sense of the situation upon them. Mrs. Scott then prayed, with not a quiver in her voice.

Two days after receiving the news, Clara wrote to close friends:

When the telegram came Thursday evening saying that John and Betty were with the Lord we did not mourn as those who have no hope, but could not but feel that a great blessing might come to the cause of Christ here in China and also wherever their martyrdom might be known. We cannot but rejoice that they have been accounted worthy to suffer for His sake, and we cannot be sorry for them that thus early they have been released from all earthly trials and have entered into the glory provided for those who belong wholly to Him. They are not the ones to have sought release from working longer in this world of darkness, but the Lord must have been satisfied that their work here was completed, and that their willingness to die for Him will bring in a larger harvest of souls than as if they had lived many years longer. It has been brought to our hearts by many Chinese and foreign friends that the kernel of wheat that dies will bear much fruit—that it cannot fall to the ground in vain, and that two kernels will bear more fruit than one.

Clara added regarding the safety of her granddaughter, after discovering the news through another telegram December 14:

To me, it is nothing less than a miracle that Baby Helen Priscilla has been spared. My husband said this morning, "All the hordes of wicked Communists couldn't harm that helpless babe, if it were the Lord's purpose to have her live to glorify His name and show His power." We know that even more He could have delivered Betty and John from their captors, had that been His will for them. We feel that the care and bringing up of this precious life is a blessed responsibility, and will need the prayers of you all to help us in this great privilege.

Hundreds of expressions offering comfort and appreciation were given to Dr. and Mrs. Scott for their daughter's work. By mail they received letters from around the world, including Australia, New Zealand, Germany, Sweden, the Arabian Peninsula, Canada, Hong Kong, England, and the United States. Kenneth, the youngest Scott sibling, wrote from Davidson College in North Carolina:

> Many people would call our loss of Betty and John a terrible tragedy that should fill us with misery and despair. But I do not see it in this way, because I am a Christian and can see God's hand behind it all. Instead of throwing us into despondency, it fills us with a greater trust in God, and a greater determination to serve Him with our lives. We do not see the meaning of it all, now, but some day we shall understand.
>
> In God's work the value of a life lived for Him is measured not by length but by quality of service, and by the fulfillment of His purposes for that life. Surely His purposes were fulfilled in Betty and John, and are being fulfilled: so their service was completed.

"When our Chinese Christians heard about John and Betty's death they wept bitterly," wrote Grace Birch to John's parents. "Though John and Betty's time in China was short, it was not in vain. They were such fine consecrated people that their death has made an extra great impression both on foreigners and Chinese. The large missionary community here in Wuhu, some of whom are modernists has been greatly stirred. The Chinese Christians in Suancheng and those in other places in southern Anhwei have been greatly touched. The people in Miaosheo where John and Betty laid down their lives were much moved by their quiet, brave courage and the fact that John even had a smile on his face when it was all over was to them a great testimony."

Previously hidden over the past two weeks due to the continued fighting in the region, the Stam's coffins were transported from Miaosheo under military escort, arriving in Wuhu on December 29. Dr. Robert Brown opened the caskets at the hospital. Two of the Stams' friends, Gordon and Marvin Dunn, missionary brothers from Canada, the latter of whom traveled to China with John, helped identify the corpses for government leaders. George Birch, Erwin Kohfield, and Nathan Walton were also present as witnesses. Gordon Dunn recalled the viewing decades afterward:

> When the coffins were finally delivered to the missionary hospital in Wuhu, the heavy coffin lids were lifted to reveal the bodies, lying on their backs, modestly clothed in their underwear, just as they had trod the streets of Tsingteh. What struck each of us who saw the bodies and what made the sight unforgettable was the underlying look of quiet peace and expectancy on the faces of the two martyrs.

Several memorials both in China and the United States occurred to commemorate the Stams' life. Following an afternoon service in the chapel of the Methodist hospital, the bodies were laid to rest on January 2, 1935, in the Wuhu foreign cemetery. Representatives of both the Nanking and United States governments were present, in addition to Betty's father and friends who served alongside the couple. Words were spoken about John and Betty, as well as tributes given to Pastor Lo, Chang Hsiu-sheng, and the released prisoner whose life was taken. The Stams' headstone, placed later that year, read:

John Cornelius Stam, January 18, 1907
"That Christ may be magnified whether by life or by death."
Philippians 1:20

Elisabeth Scott Stam, his wife, February 22, 1906
"For me to live is Christ and to die is gain."
Philippians 1:21

December 8, 1934, Miaosheo, Anhwei
"Be thou faithful unto death and I will give thee a crown of life."
Revelation 2:10

From the Anhwei Province, William Hanna commented on the attitude among John and Betty's colleagues who were left to carry on the work in China: "We thank God for the steadfastness of our fellow workers during those trying days. Not one hesitant or despondent note has been heard, but all remain constant and true—'rejoicing in hope; patient in tribulation; continuing instant in prayer.'"

A fellow missionary said of their death in a letter to Betty's parents: "We all go Home in some way! Your dear daughter and her husband have gone in a chariot of fire. . . . Now, full of vigor, their lives, their personalities, their work, their witnessing are known in every town and city of our land. A life which had the longest span of years might not have been able to do one-hundredth of the work for Christ which they had done in a day."

Charles Scott wrote of Pastor Lo and Chang Hsiu-sheng's ability to face the danger: "They illustrate Paul's grand aphorism: 'God hath not given us the spirit of fear but of power, and of love, and of a sound mind.' It is one thing to talk of Christian courage in the snug safety of our comfortable homes; it is quite another for those men and the others so nobly associated with them to count their lives dear unto themselves, for Christ's sake."

On January 18, 1935, the school's day of prayer, and what would have been John's twenty-eighth birthday, Dr. Will H. Houghton, president of Moody Bible Institute, spoke at chapel regarding the school's eleventh and twelfth missionary martyrs:

> Two of our splendid young graduates laid down their lives for the gospel in China, but this does not mean that other graduates from Moody will be deterred from going. We accept this challenge to our Christian young people of America, and will send into Christian service two hundred to take the places of the two that were slain.

At the end of Moody's chapel that day, over seven hundred young men and women stood, expressing their willingness to fill the spots of John and Betty in service to wherever God led. At nearby Wheaton College in Wheaton, Illinois, two hundred students offered themselves in similar fashion for the cause.

James M. Gray, who had recently stepped down as president of Moody, wrote to John's parents in Paterson:

> It is needless to tell you of the high standing attained by your son and his wife in our student body, where they will be long and tenderly remembered for the witness they bore to Christ by their lives as well as their lips. . . .

> I trust that already in the poignancy of your grief you have had the strength to lift your eyes to the glory that awaited them, as beyond the veil they met their Savior for whom they died. No higher honor on earth could come to parents than that which is now yours, and I pray that you are walking today in the holy joy of it.

In early 1940, Moody issued a three-year scholarship offer for Helen if she desired to attend when old enough. At Betty's alma mater, Wilson College, there was not a dry eye at the memorial. Many of the students reflected that it was the most spiritually impressive service they ever experienced. The college's president, Ethelbert Warfield, had been sick for weeks, but found the strength to give the address. Trembling to the podium from the front row, and with a voice full of emotion, Warfield spoke of his admiration for Betty and her baby. The governing board at Wilson announced that they would adopt Helen as "the College Baby," pledging the cost of her entire tuition along with a hundred dollars sent to China if the offer was taken. The school's registrar immediately entered her for the class of 1956, giving Helen the unique distinction of being the youngest person in the world to be registered into an American college.

A memorial service was held at the Star of Hope Mission in Paterson on February 21, 1935. The Mission auditorium's six hundred seats were filled, and a loudspeaker was connected to a church across the street to reach the overflow outside, making the estimated number of people who heard the tributes total over a thousand. Some of those who spoke included Jacob Stam, Geraldine Taylor, and Dr. Robert H. Glover, among others.

Geraldine Taylor went on to write *The Triumph of John and Betty Stam*, the first full-length account of their story, and a book that has produced numerous reissues over the decades since. The project was first announced at the Star of Hope service upon cooperation of the Stam and Scott families. Around the same time as Taylor was writing her book, a medical missionary in China named Lee Huizenga who maintained a connection to two brothers, Peter and Bernard Zondervan, knew his friends were looking for a gripping story for their publishing ministry, which had only been established four years prior. With an introduction by Will H. Houghton and foreword by Jacob Stam, *John and Betty Stam: Martyrs* became one of Zondervan's bestselling books when published in November 1935. The interest surrounding the couple significantly increased as a result of these two books.

At a series of evangelistic meetings held in Nanking, a Chinese woman came forward to accept Christ after hearing about the death of John and Betty. A missionary friend showed her a photo of the couple. After gazing into the picture for a long time, with tears rolling down her face, she said, "I am a new believer in Jesus. I have no acquaintances in heaven. When I get there, I want to be sure to recognize them, for they loved my people so dearly. I know that they will be my friends and will introduce me to Jesus!"

Lewis Sperry Chafer commented on the news circulating the global church: "The papers everywhere have given so much space to it, and here in Dallas called upon the people to recognize the wonderful Christian character of those who could die, pointing out, too, that not all the spirit of martyrdom has been extinguished. They have glorified God in a most wonderful way, and have called attention to the reality of a Christian testimony more definitely than perhaps they could have done in a whole lifetime of faithful service."

Walter Lingle, president of Davidson College, similarly reflected: "There is no more thrilling story in the annals of martyrdom than the story of Elisabeth Scott Stam and her husband, John C. Stam. Some may feel that here was a waste of two precious young lives. Not so. Wherever this story goes, and it has already gone to the ends of the earth, it will stir new Christian impulses and quicken new missionary zeal."

Distinguished Presbyterian Dr. Robert Speer, whose own son Elliot was murdered in September 1934, wrote to the Scott family: "We can only rejoice that our children are now beyond all the pain and anguish of our mortal life in the midst of the love and the light and the joy of God. You will have a sacred charge now in the little one, just as we feel we have in Elliot's three little girls."

During the following months of 1935, gifts came from around the world for Helen Priscilla to both sides of her family, with enough clothing to last multiple years. By the end of January of that year, over twenty people, including several couples from around the world, had already volunteered to adopt her, with many more offers to follow. Charles and Clara Scott decided to take it upon themselves to raise their granddaughter in China, not wanting others to take advantage of the publicity. Nevertheless, in the course of her early years growing up, Helen became a celebrity child who captured the media's imagination. Everyone from Chinese Christians, missionaries, and visitors all wanted to see the girl known as "the Miracle Baby." Each passing year, newspapers and magazines requested photos and updates to present the progress of Helen's youth. For Christians around the world, she became a household name, while for many nonbelievers she was a face of hope in America; a descendant of John and Priscilla Alden who was able to escape the grasp of communist China.

"Nearly one hundred boys and girls of our Sunday School are praying for Helen Priscilla every day, and the children have each contributed to buy the little baby dresses which we are sending her," wrote a Methodist pastor in Oregon. Another tale goes that when a pastor in London, England, was walking in the garden of his vicarage one day a little girl unexpectedly came in and asked, "Will you please tell me how Helen Priscilla is now?"

Helen lived with her maternal grandparents until summer 1939, when the Second Sino-Japanese War forced a one-year furlough, sending the three of them out of the country enroute from Shanghai to Vancouver. Shortly after arriving back to America, tensions arose between the Stam and Scott families regarding who would raise Helen. With permission from her maternal grandparents, she stayed her year of kindergarten with Henry Stam and his family in New Jersey. However, the mutual family disputes over how to handle the delicate situation of an orphaned girl known around the world was challenging for members on both sides, as Helen's fame had only grown since coming to the States. Another difficulty was a series of nervous breakdowns

Peter Stam had had over the past number of years, resulting in his having to be institutionalized for brief periods. Two of these breakdowns came after John and Betty died. On the morning of June 10, 1940, Peter fell instantly to his death from a bathroom window on the second floor of the Stam home in Paterson. Helen Priscilla, trying to make sense of her parents' death and what she meant to so many at almost six years old, lost a grandfather she was just getting to know. While enduring the continued pressure being celebrated as the miracle child and feeling closer to the Scott side after that year, she would officially be adopted and raised by her aunt Helen and uncle George Mahy Jr.

In relation to the aftermath of John and Betty's martyrdom, even through grief and hardship, the remaining siblings of the Stam and Scott families all carried on serving the Lord they loved the rest of their days. Many continued as missionaries abroad while others worked in respective ministries or educational institutions in the States. Several churches associated with the related families commemorated John and Betty's life around the anniversary of their death, further spreading their testimony. This story of two lives told around the world would not only have an influence for generations to come, but at the time brought together a body of believers as one, the likes of which had never been seen before.

The February 1935 edition of *China's Millions* included a lengthy tribute to the mission's seventy-third and seventy-fourth martyrs. The tribute concluded with these enduring words:

> It has been a long time since any event connected with the mission field has made so wide and profound an impression on this country. We believe that John and Betty Stam may by their death have spoken even more loudly than by their brief lives of devoted service. Let no one call this ending of their earthly career a tragedy, for in reality it is a triumph. It recalls to our mind the old seal of the noble Moravian Brotherhood consisting of a lamb upon a crimson background, together with the cross of resurrection and a banner of victory. Underneath all was the motto in Latin which translated into English, reads: OUR LAMB HAS CONQUERED; LET US FOLLOW HIM. John and Betty Stam were true followers of the lamb—in life, and even unto death. Again, the challenge comes: "Who follows in their train?"

TIME Magazine
Monday, Dec. 24, 1934
CHINA: Undercurrent of Joy

A Paterson, N. J. evangelist had a letter last week from his missionary son in China. John C. Stam wrote of the menace of Communist-bandits and enclosed a poem which, he said, expressed his own feelings about them:

Afraid? Of what?
Afraid to see the Savior's face?
To pass from pain to perfect grace?
The glory gleam from wound of grace?
Afraid—of that?

By the time Father Stam read the letter, Son John and Son John's wife had, in fact, "passed from pain" at the hands of Chinese Communist-bandits.

Typical of the plain-living, courageous line of U. S. missionaries in China were the John C. Stams. Both children of Protestant churchmen, they looked remarkably alike: serious, firm-jawed young people with tortoise-shell glasses. Married 14 months ago, Mrs. Stam had her first child, a girl, by a caesarean operation, last September. Outposters of the interdenominational China Inland Mission, they taught the way of the Lord in Tsingteh in Southern Anhwei Province, 200 miles from Nanking, which is Generalissimo Chiang Kai-Shek's stronghold of law & order.

Last month Generalissimo Chiang announced that he had "broken the backbone of Communism in China" by chasing the Communists out of Kiangsi Province. Nanking authorities added that nearby districts were "safe." Nonetheless, a band of Communists bobbed up at Tsingteh and kidnapped Mr. and Mrs. Stam and Daughter Helen Priscilla. One morning last week the Communists paraded the two missionaries through the muddy streets of a nearby village, then slashed off their heads with a great curved sword, supposedly in a shrewd effort to embarrass Generalissimo Chiang. A Chinese Christian pastor found the Stams' baby girl alive in a deserted house, a $10 bill and several clean diapers tucked inside her blanket. Chinese mothers volunteered milk until the infant could be taken to the Wuhu hospital where she was born three months ago.

Genuinely embarrassed, the Generalissimo sent 10,000 soldiers boiling after the murderers last week. And in Paterson, N. J. Mr. Stam's brother Jacob said: "We know we will see our dear ones in Heaven, and while there are tears there is an undercurrent of joy, because we know the way of the Lord. They were worthy to be in His service and they were worthy to die a martyr's death."

From TIME. © 1934 TIME USA LLC. All rights reserved. Used under license.

CHAPTER FOURTEEN

Legacy

The two prominent books published about the Stams in 1935 made a tremendous influence on young and old alike to serve in Christian ministry or reaffirm their faith. John and Betty's legacy can be summed up in the countless people affected by a lifetime's worth of recognition and testimony.

Elisabeth Howard, who as a four-year-old met Betty Scott, recognized the couple when her father brought home a newspaper one evening in January 1935, speaking of their deaths. The front page contained two photos: the first of John and Betty and the other of baby Helen being brought to the Wuhu hospital. This event sustained a defining moment in eight-year-old Elisabeth Howard as she began to realize what complete surrender looked like, thinking how this same woman had sat at her family's dinner table. Two decades later, after graduating from Wheaton College a year apart, Elisabeth and her future husband, Jim Elliot, served as missionaries in Ecuador. Jim and his four colleagues were speared to death by local indigenous tribesmen on January 8, 1956. Two years later, Elisabeth Elliot (wife of Jim) and Rachel Saint (sister of Nate Saint) returned to live among the Huaorani people and learn their language.

The mission effort was successful, with many in the tribe coming to know the gospel message and turning from their violent past.

For those not familiar, the story itself compelled a new generation of believers to missionary service, while Elisabeth Elliot poured herself into writing books and conducting speaking engagements about the faith that shaped her. Elliot often cited Betty Scott Stam and Amy Carmichael, missionary to India, as her inspiration. She copied by hand Betty Scott's prayer into her Bible at age twelve, and later in life often gave out small printed copies to those she felt needed it, reminding them that the gospel was to be shared at any cost.

Chuck Smith, founder of Calvary Chapel, and who maintained a large presence during the Jesus movement, shared the Stams' story with his daughter Cheryl during her early teens:

> My father was headed somewhere, and I jokingly asked him to bring me back something special. After his return he handed me *The Triumph of John and Betty Stam*. He proceeded to tell me that this book had been one of his favorite stories. He happened to see it, wherever he was, and bought it for me. Later after I finished reading it, I remember talking with him about their martyrdom and how depressing it was for me (keep in mind my age at the time). He remarked that that was one of the reasons he loved the title, "The Triumph" . . . because it showed their faithfulness unto death.

Theologian and pastor John Piper wrote of reading the same book and being moved by their devotion to Christ: "Every time I read it, the compounding of the preciousness and the pain by the marriage and the baby make me weep. The rending depth of emotion in such a moment overwhelms me. The shame of being stripped, the terror of the pain, the hideous sorrow of seeing a lover beheaded, the last thought of little Helen abandoned."

John and Betty Stam: Martyrs left an impression on sixteen-year-old Kansas native John W. Peterson, who went on to become one of the most prominent gospel songwriters of the twentieth century. Reflecting on discovering the text one Saturday morning in his bedroom, he told in his 1976 autobiography *The Miracle Goes On*:

> As I turned the last page in that book, something broke inside me. How could it be, Lord, that this bright, promising young couple should be cut down at the very outset of their ministry? Why? To what purpose? Was this what commitment was all about—to come to the end of oneself and lay one's life on the line for Christ, regardless of the consequences? . . .

> I began to weep in anguish as I prayed: Surely, Lord, You wouldn't ask that of me—that I go to China and die for You? I could do so much more for you here . . . it can't be that You want me to put myself so completely into Your hands! . . .

Aboard the *Empress of Japan* traveling to China: (from left; top) John Stam, Marvin Dunn, Arthur Diefenbaker, Bengt Hallgren; (bottom) Will Windsor, Albert Grant, Connie Windsor, Percy Clark, Marjorie Windsor (child), late September–early October 1932 (Photo courtesy of Ian Grant)

Portrait of John and Betty in Shanghai, November 11, 1933

Wedding party inside the Scott home, October 25, 1933: (from left) Katie Dodd, Percy
Bramley, Marguerite Luce, Betty Stam, John Stam, Nancy Rodgers

John and Betty Stam's wedding, October 25, 1933: (from left) Katie Dodd, Percy Bramley, Marguerite Luce, R. A. Torrey Jr., Betty Stam, John Stam, Clara Scott, Charles Scott, Nancy Rodgers (Wheaton Archives)

Inside one of Betty's diaries, recovered from the Stams' looted home, was a single piece of loose film. When developed and enlarged after the Scotts returned to America in 1939, the film revealed this photo of a happy John and Betty on their honeymoon in Tsingtao, late October 1933.

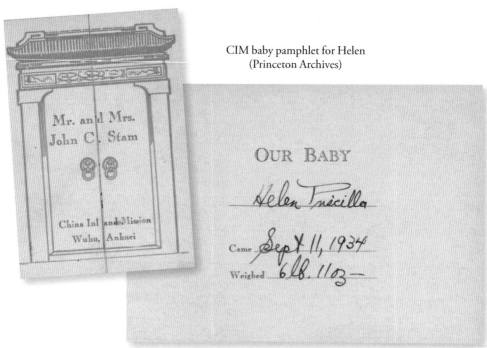

CIM baby pamphlet for Helen
(Princeton Archives)

Mr. and Mrs.
John C. Stam

China Inland Mission
Wuhu, Anhuei

OUR BABY

Helen Priscilla

Came Sept 11, 1934

Weighed 6 lb. 11 oz —

John Stam's handwritten details inside pamphlet

John holding Helen in the Wuhu
hospital shortly after her birth,
mid-September 1934

Photo taken by John outside the walls
of Tsingteh while visiting with Erwin Kohfield,
late October 1934

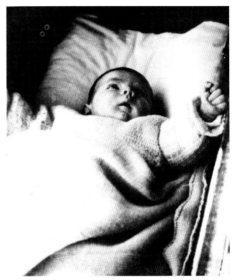

Helen, photographed by John,
early November 1934

Last photo of Betty, taken by John,
early November 1934
(Princeton Archives)

Helen and Pastor Lo's son being carried in rice baskets by servant (name unknown) to Wuhu hospital, December 15, 1934; (from left) Pastor Lo, Charlotte Hsia (nurse), George Birch, Mrs. Lo, Robert Brown (Photo by Howard Smith)

Outside the Wuhu hospital, December 15, 1934
(from left): Pastor Lo, servant, George Birch, Charlotte Hsia holding Helen (Photo by Howard Smith)

Helen Priscilla Stam, December 15, 1934. Perhaps the most widely published
missions photo of the twentieth century (Photo by Howard Smith)

Missionaries in Wuhu, December 15, 1934 (from left): David Birch, Grace Birch holding John Birch, George Birch, Nathan Walton holding Barbara Ann Walton, Lois Walton, Laura Woosley, Helen Stam being held by William Hanna, Mrs. Hanna (Photo by Howard Smith)

George Birch and Helen,
December 15, 1934
(Photo by Howard Smith)

Pastor Lo and Helen,
December 15, 1934
(Photo by Howard Smith)

John's and Betty's coffins arriving in Wuhu under military escort, December 29, 1934
(Photo by Howard Smith)

Military officials and missionary friends after unloading the coffins, December 29, 1934
(Photo by Howard Smith)

John and Betty's grave,
summer 1935
(Photo by Howard Smith)

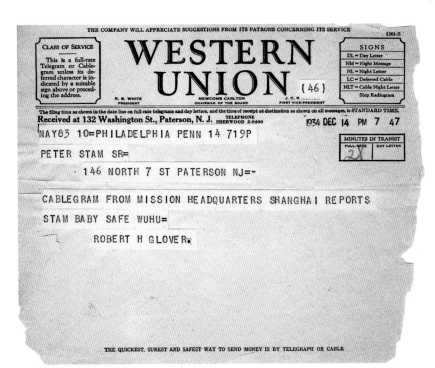

Original telegram sent to Stam family reporting Helen's survival (Wheaton Archives)

Helen with Chinese children, early 1935 (Wheaton Archives)

Charles Scott and Helen, March 11, 1935

Helen at the Scotts' home in Tsinan, September 30, 1935 (Princeton Archives)

Helen in China at almost three years old, 1937

Helen on her fifth birthday with Stam cousins, Lois and Ruth Brain, September 11, 1939

Helen on her fifth birthday, September 11, 1939 (MBI Archives)

Helen with her Stam grandparents, May 22, 1940

Ruth, Cornelius, and Clazina Stam at Holland Christian
Home in Haledon, New Jersey, May 16, 1981

Ruth (second from left)
with sons of Peter Stam Jr.:
Peter Stam III (left), John Stam (right)
with his wife, Bonnie;
inside Cornelius Stam's study
in Chicago, May 20, 1990

Andrew Montonera,
Kathy (Frizane) Montonera,
Grace Frizane, and Cornelius Stam,
February 2, 2002

Family with great-grandparents on Mother's Day,
May 10, 1998. Grandmother Grace (Wahlstrom) Frizane
is holding baby Andrew Montonera

Andrew Montonera and
Cornelius Stam, February 2, 2002

Hours passed, but I was unconscious of time. My tears had long since dried, for I was beginning to understand that if I wanted God to use my life (and I did), it was necessary for my life to be under His Lordship, His control, free of the pitfalls of blind chance and personal ambition. . . .

At length the last wall of my resistance crumbled, and I promised Him: Here I am, Lord. I don't know what You want of me, but even if it's China and martyrdom, I'm willing.

Toward evening an inexpressible joy and peace filled my heart. . . . When I finally tore myself away and went downstairs, the day had passed, and evening had come. The family had long since finished dinner, but mother had kept some food warm for me. In her face I saw the understanding that something of unusual importance had kept me closeted all day in my room. She must have sensed that I had gone through a spiritual battle and that the Lord had won.

Award-winning songwriter and producer Wayne Kirkpatrick, whose songs have been heard and sung around the world, said, "My dad founded a church in Denham Springs, Louisiana, just outside of Baton Rouge called Berean Bible Fellowship back in the late 1970s and pastored it for twenty-five years until his retirement. He was heavily influenced by the writings of Cornelius Stam. Years later my wife and I were made aware of John and Betty."

Irish music duo Keith and Kristyn Getty shared:

The legacy of John and Betty Stam's missionary service and martyrdom powerfully challenges us in our own discipleship and continually inspires our hymn writing ministry. Through having had the blessing of knowing Carl "Chip" Stam, one of Jacob Stam's grandsons, we received a deeper personal connection to the Christ-like example of John and Betty, and find our faith invigorated as we consider their example. The Stams' story has motivated us to be ever more conscious of the urgent need for the body of Christ to obey the Great Commission in our generation. Given our esteem for the Stams, we are deeply honored to have had the opportunity to record and re-introduce Frank Houghton's hymns "Facing a Task Unfinished" and "Thou Who Wast Rich Beyond All Splendor," the latter of which was inspired by the Stams' martyrdom. We believe the preceding to be the greatest missional hymn of the twentieth century, and we pray that as believers, families and churches sing these songs, they would be motivated to continue to "bear the torch that flaming, fell from the hands of those who gave their lives proclaiming that Jesus died and rose."

Erwin Lutzer, Pastor Emeritus of the Moody Church in Chicago, said, "When I taught at Moody Bible Institute in the '70s and then was appointed Senior Pastor of Moody Church, I became acquainted with the story of John and Betty Stam, and soon realized the ongoing impact of their martyrdom. How encouraging it is to be reminded that Moody Bible Institute played a part in their lives, preparing the two for the ultimate sacrifice of giving themselves for the gospel. It is just like God to take a terrible tragedy which at the time seemed like such a loss, and use it to inspire and remind future generations, all that really matters is what lasts forever."

John and Betty became known to evangelist Billy Graham. His wife, Ruth, was raised in China and her father, L. Nelson Bell, was friends with both the Stam and Scott families. During his later years, Jacob Stam worked as a lawyer for the Billy Graham Evangelistic Association, and a few months before his own death, Bell gave the eulogy at Clara Scott's memorial service in spring 1973. From the children of Billy and Ruth:

> The whole Graham family has a deep appreciation for John and Betty Stam. Early in life we heard stories of the Stams. They were talked about around our dinner table; held up as heroes and examples of serving Jesus. Our grandparents, Dr. and Mrs. L. Nelson Bell, also missionaries in China, admired and respected them for their firm commitment to serve the Lord Jesus among the Chinese people. And of course, Mother, Ruth Bell Graham, wanted to follow in their footsteps—however, to Tibet. They were her role models. Father, though not a missionary and never met John or Betty, grew to admire them through our mother and grandparents.

Many of the Stams' friends lived out their call for the advance of the gospel throughout China and beyond. The Birch family faithfully continued their work in the country until December 1944. John Birch, who was dedicated alongside Helen Priscilla as an infant, would grow up in China and eventually attend Chefoo, the CIM's boarding school, with his older brother, David. The school was captured by Japanese troops after the attack on Pearl Harbor, and together the brothers spent three and a half years as prisoners of war, with the last two in the Weihsien Internment Camp. Weihsien is probably best remembered as the camp where missionary and famed Olympic runner Eric Liddell spent his final years, and both boys were able to develop a close relationship with him during that same period.

After the camp's liberation, John and David returned to Canada in November 1945. During John's first year of medical school at the University of British Columbia, while driving on a local highway, his motorcycle was struck by a drunk driver, instantly killing John on September 25, 1954. He was only twenty years old.

"John believed God was guiding him to a lifetime of service as a medical missionary," says the youngest Birch son, Art. "He was an excellent student at UBC, a cross-country runner, and a leader of Christian students on campus. As a boy of seven, standing at his graveside, I felt God was calling me to take his place. I grew up believing I would be a medical missionary. At age twenty, God redirected my steps to pastoral ministry, but I have known since John's passing that I am God's servant, as are all His children."

A friend even younger than Art felt so inspired to take John's place that he later became a doctor and missionary in Pakistan. David Birch, who grew up knowing the Stams as "Uncle John" and "Aunt Betty," passed away in 2019. George and Grace Birch always felt blessed to have known John and Betty while serving together, and to this day the entire family is still grateful to be associated with the rescue of baby Helen.

God used the Stams' lives to glorify Him while also directly changing the way international missions could be perceived on a global scale. Since their martyrdom, Christianity has only continued to flourish in China. The exact number of believers today is unknown due to the overwhelming control of the government, but the stories that have come out of the country and greater Asia have been a fruitful testament in a land that faces so much persecution. Their lives have endured through a ripple effect of changed hearts around the world. Perhaps the most unique and inspiring situation follows into the twenty-first century.

When James Hudson Taylor IV visited China in 2006, he went searching for the location of John and Betty's burial. The cemetery and Stams' gravestone had been destroyed decades prior by communists during the Cultural Revolution to suppress any history of foreign missionaries, but the site of their burial still exists around a small garden in downtown Wuhu. After speaking with many of the local Chinese Christians, he came to discover they were not very familiar with the Stams due to the suppression of Christian martyrdom in China. After their death was shared with many of the locals, they questioned why they'd been ignorant of the spiritual heritage in a land that so thirsts for the gospel. With help from a Chinese Christian couple from America named Pine and Esther Wang, word began spreading further about the Stams' love for their people.

In 2009, the Wangs, along with some others who had come to know the account from Taylor's visit, located a ninety-year-old man in a Chinese village who might be able to give some insight on the Stams. For fear of his life, he'd never spoken before of the events he witnessed when he was just fifteen. Reluctant at first, the man proceeded to say, "I'm an old man, what can the government do to me now?" He went on to explain how seventy-five years before, John Stam would come to Miaosheo to play games and teach him about a man named Jesus. For the duration of his life, he never understood why this young couple was marched through the middle of the village as people of all ages were forced to see these "foreign devils." On that day he watched as Chang Hsiu-sheng pleaded for the Stams' lives, and then huddled up against a pine tree on Eagle Hill as he shook with fear witnessing their execution. Esther Wang shared the gospel with "Uncle Dong," as they knew him, and asked if he'd like to become a follower of Jesus Christ. He replied, "Yes," and they prayed together. A small piece of this seed planted over seven decades earlier had come to blossom. "Uncle Dong" died a few years later, but a person of faith can imagine John Stam reuniting with a soul he dedicated his life to serve.

Outside Moody Bible Institute's chapel is a wall display that lists all the missionaries from the school since their founding. An asterisk next to the names mark those who died for their commitment to living out the Great Commission. How can we ever know the full impact of a testimony by laying down one's life? Eternity alone will tell. For John and Betty Stam, they wished to honor God wherever He led, whether in this life or the next. On December 8, 1934, passing on to the other side and encountering their Savior face to face was the ultimate reward they could ask for. The love for each other, friendships, ambitions, comforts, and daily needs were all taken to their heavenly Father on this end. Faithfulness carried them through.

A Note from the Author

Helen Priscilla lived out the majority of her youth as a mission-ary kid with her adoptive parents in China and the Philippines before returning to America where she finished her senior year of high school. Coming back to the States, Helen chose a private life away from the spotlight—no public interviews or appearances regarding her parents, along with disassociating from the media's sensationalized per-sona. She attended and graduated from Wilson College just as her mother and two aunts did. However, Helen gave up the tuition offered as an infant to go toward "someone deserving" because she won a scholarship to Wilson by ranking eighth in her graduating high school class and winning a competitive exam. She then studied at the Presbyterian School of Christian Education in Richmond, Virginia, while also serving in campus ministry.

At a Stam family reunion in the early 1980s, my great-grandmother sat next to Helen and the two spent some time talking together. Neil and Ruth had a more intimate visit with her not long after where they shared several family memories. Neil and his first wife, Henrietta, were one of the couples who initially offered to adopt Helen as they couldn't have children of their own. During the early research phase, I briefly spoke on the phone with Helen and was able to introduce myself as the great-grandson of Cornelius and Ruth Stam; she declined to participate in this book. In the end, I was grateful for the chance to speak with the individual closest on this journey of rediscovery. With tears gently running down my cheek and a choked-up voice I expressed how, even though I'm only distantly related, her parents' story has meant so much to me. The words of sincerity were reaffirmed.

For several years following their death, Neil was often asked to speak on the East Coast about the martyrdom of his brother and sister-in-law, which eventually bothered him. Later in life he told our family about those early years, saying, "Finally I simply had to explain that I had been called of God to preach Christ, to declare the riches of the grace of Him who first died for John and Betty Stam and that I was sure they would have it so. With rare exceptions they understood, and I did just that."

When my great-grandparents moved to the retirement community of Windsor Park Manor in the summer of 1993, many of the residents associated them with the Stam name because of John and Betty, and several soon wanted to plan a time to have dinner together. One incredible, almost providential circumstance is that two of those people were Otto Schoerner and Katie Dodd, who both attended Moody and served alongside John and Betty in China. The two eventually got married while missionaries in 1937, and had moved into the same retirement facility after Christmas 1993. I like to believe this was God's way of letting Neil reminisce that a piece of his immediate family would continue to be there during his final years. He even kept a small thank-you note from the couple after he let them borrow one of his books about the Stams.

I stumbled across the collection of books recovered from John and Betty's home again in the summer of 2021, the same ones my grandmother showed me as a boy. I thought in the moment, "Why is it, God, that You allowed these to end up in my hands?" I'm looking at them now, collecting dust on a bookshelf a few feet away in a warm comfortable room in suburban America. Thinking about how John glanced at these same books in his home one last time after being captured and still being able to collectively say none of it matters—God is in control. How they sat alone in silence as a three-month-old clung to the breasts of strangers to stay alive, all while her slain parents provided what they could, and how that little girl's own father went home a saved teenager next to my Grandpa Stam. If pages could speak, they might tell of those brave hearts, along with the courage and peace which possessed their souls.

In my view, the Stams' life fulfilled their calling. Everything they challenged the world with was accomplished in an instant. As I write this, I'm around the age John and Betty were when preparing to leave for the mission field. And while I don't see myself becoming an overseas missionary, I am able to relate to some degree as I've experienced my own suffering in personal loss of life and relationships with others over the past few years alone. I've begun to see how God intertwines moments of time that play a role in sharing His creation and greater kingdom. John and Betty could have never imagined their life would be cut so short, or that others might be forever changed by their story; but both also believed in a God who used ordinary people through His divine will to accomplish amazing things. The Stams allowed us to identify with them through most, if not every, capable raw emotion. Part of the human experience is wrestling with the wonders of a gracious Father who gives and takes away. Yet as difficult and painful as it sometimes is, God expects us each day to give our best to Him. I have never known a day the sun has not risen. As I evaluate my own life, may God be placed above those desires and fears of this fractured world.

I don't know what God has for my future, I don't know what He has for yours, but I do know this: I know that He is good, and that His plans assemble in ways we cannot always comprehend. As I get older, I have seen in more ways than one how family comes together as a part of God's plan in our heritage, both physical and spiritual. I hope this rings true for the many other Stam and Scott relatives, most of whom I have not met. The impact that can be made for future generations should never be underestimated as we live out our days, because the simplest things often make us look toward a life beyond this realm.

I'm ultimately grateful to God for letting my family catch a glimpse of the Stams' testimony in our lives, as I certainly know the impact they have had on mine. I pray that God leads me in His sovereignty each day, helps me remember this world is temporary, and just as John Stam was reminded, it's Him that girdeth me with strength.

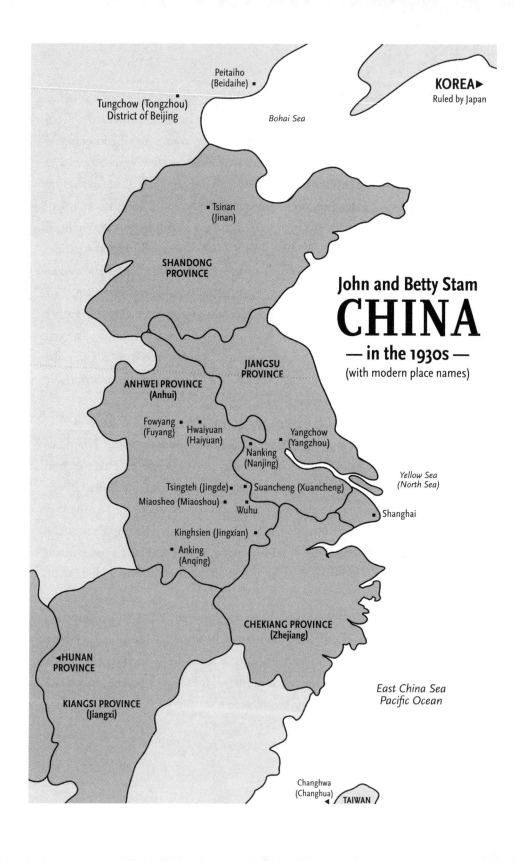

Peitaiho
(Beidaihe)

Tungchow (Tongzhou)
District of Beijing

Bohai Sea

KOREA▶
Ruled by Japan

■ Tsinan
(Jinan)

**SHANDONG
PROVINCE**

John and Betty Stam
CHINA
— in the 1930s —
(with modern place names)

**JIANGSU
PROVINCE**

**ANHWEI PROVINCE
(Anhui)**

Fowyang ■
(Fuyang)   ■ Hwaiyuan
              (Haiyuan)
         ■ Nanking
         (Nanjing)

Yangchow ■
(Yangzhou)

*Yellow Sea
(North Sea)*

Tsingteh (Jingde) ■   ■ Suancheng (Xuancheng)
Miaosheo (Miaoshou) ■
              ■ Wuhu   ■ Shanghai

Kinghsien (Jingxian) ■

■ Anking
(Anqing)

**CHEKIANG PROVINCE
(Zhejiang)**

◀HUNAN
PROVINCE

*East China Sea
Pacific Ocean*

**KIANGSI PROVINCE
(Jiangxi)**

Changhwa
(Changhua)
◀ **TAIWAN**

APPENDIX: JOHN AND BETTY STAM FAMILY

Stam Family

Peter Stam: May 23, 1866–June 10, 1940 (age 74)

Amelia E. A. Williams: October 31, 1867–August 3, 1961 (age 93)

Married: January 7, 1892

Children

Peter Stam Jr.: November 9, 1892–February 11, 1986 (age 93)

Clazina J. Stam: December 22, 1894–February 27, 1998 (age 103)

Henry N. Stam: January 5, 1897–April 3, 1969 (age 72)

Jacob (Jake) Stam: September 18, 1899–April 19, 1972 (age 72)

Harry Stam: December 30, 1901–January 4, 1983 (age 81)

Catherine Stam: May 24, 1904–April 4, 1905 (age 10 months)

John C. Stam: January 18, 1907–December 8, 1934 (age 27)

Cornelius (Neil) R. Stam: May 27, 1908–March 9, 2003 (age 94)

Amelia (Babe) G. Stam: November 11, 1911–March 19, 2002 (age 90)

Scott Family

Charles E. Scott: June 22, 1876–November 25, 1961 (age 85)

Clara E. Heywood: August 3, 1878–May 26, 1973 (age 94)

Married: September 9, 1903

Children

Elisabeth (Betty) A. Scott: February 22, 1906–December 8, 1934 (age 28)

Helen P. Scott: September 23, 1908–March 31, 2001 (age 92)

Beatrice (Bunny) E. Scott: January 9, 1911–May 12, 2010 (age 99)

Francis (Laddie) H. Scott: December 1, 1912–September 9, 2001 (age 88)

Kenneth (Ken) M. Scott: March 22, 1916–September 15, 2014 (age 98)

ACKNOWLEDGMENTS

This book would not have been possible without the support of my family and close friends who invested in me. As with any biography, let alone for two individuals, it is always difficult to choose how to present their lives with the information given. For the result of my research and effort, I thank the following.

I corresponded with direct descendants and relatives to those listed of John and Betty's generation during the writing process: Peter Stam Jr., Jacob Stam, Henry Stam, Cornelius Stam, Amelia Stam, Kenneth Scott. I'm grateful for all of you and your contributions.

My immediate family: Ken and Grace Frizane, Ray and Kathy Montonera, Darrell and Abby Montonera; my niece and nephew: Eliana and Tobias Montonera.

My developmental editor at Moody Publishers, Kevin Mungons, for giving me the opportunity and encouragement to share this book with the world.

James Hudson Taylor IV, for writing the foreword and your complete support from the beginning.

Ray Smith, son of Howard Smith: Thank you for our conversations and sharing your knowledge of events as well as your father's incredible photography. Children of Ray Smith: Scott Smith, Heidi Truty.

Descendants of George and Grace Birch: Art Birch, Miriam Hubick, Helen Phillips, Andrew Thompson.

Ian Grant, son of Albert Grant: Thank you for the photo of John Stam and missionaries aboard the *Empress of Japan*.

The Elisabeth Elliot Foundation: Kathy Reeg, Valerie Shepard, Lars Gren, Jim Howard, Brian Lacey.

Billy Graham Evangelistic Association: David Bruce; children of Billy and Ruth Graham: Gigi, Anne, Ruth, Franklin, Ned.

The ministries and institutions who opened their archives to me. Berean

Bible Society: Kevin and Jessica Sadler, Victoria Sadler, Katelyn Sadler, Jim Tollar, Ricky Kurth; Wheaton Archives & Special Collections, Wheaton College, IL: Emily Banas, Keith Call, Katherine Graber; Crowell Library Archives, Moody Bible Institute: Corie Zylstra; Moody Bible Institute's Office of Academic Records: Bethanne Tremper; Hankey Center Archives, Wilson College: Jessica Walker; Wright Library Archives, Princeton Theological Seminary: Lydia Andeskie.

Additionally, I would like to thank: Cheryl Brodersen, Wayne and Fran Kirkpatrick, Keith and Kristyn Getty, Erwin Lutzer, John Piper, Pine and Esther Wang, Dunn family.

My personal photographer, Sarah Barlow.

Last, I'd like to dedicate this book to my grandfather, Ken Frizane, as well as my great-grandparents, Irving Wahlstrom, Ruth Wahlstrom Stam, and Cornelius Stam. Thank you for the continued spiritual heritage you instilled upon our family. I hope this book is proof for all who read it. I'm grateful for the reminder that He loves us far more than we will ever love Him. All glory to God!

PHOTO CREDITS

All photos unless otherwise noted are from the personal collection and estate of Andrew Montonera.

Photo credited to MBI Archives is used by permission of Moody Bible Institute Archives, Chicago, Illinois.

Photos credited to Wheaton Archives are used by permission of Wheaton Archives and Special Collections, Wheaton College, Wheaton, Illinois.

Photos credited to Princeton Archives are used by permission of Archives and Special Collections, Princeton Theological Seminary, Princeton, New Jersey.

Photo credited to Ian Grant is used by permission of Ian Grant.

Photos credited to Howard Smith are used by permission of Ray Smith and the Howard Smith estate.

NOTES

FOREWORD by James Hudson Taylor IV

7 **"He is no fool"**: Jim Elliot journal entry: October 28, 1949. Box 1, Folder 8, CN 277: Journal, Vol. 3; March 11, 1949–August 15, 1950. Wheaton Archives & Special Collections, Wheaton College, IL.

8 **"the blood of the martyrs"**: Tertullian, *Apologeticus pro Christianis*, 48–50.

PREFACE

12 My immediate family has always spelled Cornelius's abbreviation as *Neil*, which is why I've chosen to present it this way. Cornelius is referred to as *Neal* in chapter 1 of *The Triumph of John and Betty Stam*. In his memoirs, written in the early 1980s at the request of his wife, Ruth, Cornelius spelled his name *Neill*. Stam family members throughout the years have spelled it any of those three ways.

13 **"We have never had"**: Lewis Sperry Chafer, quoted in Clara and Charles Ernest Scott, "In Loving Memory of John and Betty—An Anniversary Letter," April 1936 (self-published circular letter), 74: The Scott Family (China Missions) Manuscript Collection. Box 1, File 1:3. Princeton Theological Seminary Archives, Princeton, NJ.

PROLOGUE: AT ANY COST

15 The events and much of the dialogue written are based on depositions made by Mei Tsong-fuh and Li Ming-chin before George Atcheson Jr., Consul of the United States of America, in and for the consular district of Nanking, China, January 1, 1935. Box 1, Folder 7, CN 449: Correspondence with Government Officials about the murders. Wheaton Archives. Also based on the accounts in Mrs. Howard [Geraldine] Taylor, *The Triumph of John and Betty Stam* (Philadelphia, PA: China Inland Mission, 1935), and Lee Sjoerds Huizenga, *John and Betty Stam: Martyrs* (Grand Rapids, MI: Zondervan, 1935).

16 **"It is better"**: Betty Stam, quoted in Taylor, *Triumph of John and Betty Stam*, 101.

17 **John Stam letter to CIM officials**: December 6, 1934. Box 1, Folder 7, CN 449. Wheaton Archives.

1. A HERITAGE FROM HOLLAND

20 **"It has two columns"**: Margaret Neighmond, quoted in Cornelius R. Stam, *The Memoirs of Pastor Cornelius R. Stam* (Germantown, WI: Berean Bible Society, 2003), 14.

20 **"The book told me"**: Peter Stam, quoted in Taylor, *Triumph of John and Betty Stam*, 2.

21 **"Then you are out"**: Employer to Peter Stam, quoted in Lee Sjoerds Huizenga, *John and Betty Stam: Martyrs* (Grand Rapids, MI: Zondervan, 1935), 26.

2. HUMBLE BEGINNINGS

23 **"We certainly were"**: Clazina Stam, quoted in Taylor, *Triumph of John and Betty Stam*, 4.

25 **"Mr. Stam, I'm so"**: Woman on phone with Peter Stam, quoted in Cornelius Stam, *Memoirs*, 29.

26 **"And thy house"**: Jacob Stam speech at CIM memorial service for John and Betty Stam, February 21, 1935. Box 1, Folder 14, CN 449: Memorial Service Transcript (1935). Wheaton Archives.

26 **"It's up to you, John"**: Peter Stam, quoted in Taylor, *Triumph of John and Betty Stam*, 8.

27 **"I am the wrong man"**: as quoted in John Stam's Testimony below.

28 **John Stam's Testimony**: John reflects on the day he got saved as "morning" when he heard Pastor Houston preach. Both Cornelius and Jacob Stam remember the event as night in their own accounts, which is how I have presented it for the story in chapter 2. Pastor Houston held services over a period of multiple days and John likely confused the small detail when reflecting on it over a decade later. A copy of this testimony can be found in Box 1, Folder 16, CN 449: John Stam Testimony. Wheaton Archives.

3. GROWING UP OVERSEAS

32 **Scotts' possessions lost in typhoon**: Kenneth M. Scott, *Around the World in Eighty Years* (Franklin, TN: Providence House Publishers, 1998), 3–4.

32 **"The Lilac"** poem: (dated November 17, 1914) Elisabeth Alden Scott Stam, *The Poems and Verse of Betty Scott Stam* (Shanghai, China: Kelly & Walsh Ltd., 1938), 3. Also published as Elisabeth Alden Scott Stam, *The Faith of Betty Scott Stam in Poems and Verse*, ed. Clara and Charles E. Scott (New York: Fleming H. Revell, 1938). The Revell edition was also published under the imprint of China Inland Mission, 1938.

33 **"I think that"**: Helen Scott, quoted in Taylor, *Triumph of John and Betty Stam*, 23.

33 **"To Father and Mother"** poem: November 21, 1929. Elisabeth Stam, *Poems and Verse*, 87–88.

36 **"Traveller's Song"** poem: dated July 14, 1925. Elisabeth Stam, *Poems and Verse*, 46. Some later publications changed Betty's original British spelling of "Traveller's" to the American "Traveler's."

37 **"All five of us"**: Helen Scott, quoted in Taylor, *Triumph of John and Betty Stam*, 26.

4. A LIFE FURTHER SURRENDERED

39 **"'Keswick' is over"**: Betty Scott to parents, Ibid., 34–35.

40 **"When we consecrate"**: Betty Scott, Ibid., 35.

41 **"Perhaps what most"**: Warren Nevius, Ibid., 34.

41 **"She chose Moody's"**: Betty's sister, Ibid., 36.

42 **"My Testimony"** poem: February 22, 1929. Elisabeth Stam, *Poems and Verse*, 80.

43 **"These are real poems"**: Henry Van Dyke Jr., quoted from Walter Lingle, "Christian Observer, Talks on Timely Topics—Our Missionary Martyrs," February 27, 1935: The Scott Family (China Missions) Manuscript Collection. Box 1, File 1:3. Princeton Archives.

43 **"Betty was by nature"**: Charles and Clara Scott in the Foreword to Elisabeth Stam, *The Poems and Verse of Betty Scott Stam* (Shanghai, China: Kelly & Walsh Ltd., 1938), n. p.

43 **"This poem expresses"**: Betty Scott to father, quoted in Taylor, *Triumph of John and Betty Stam*, 39.

43 **"Stand Still and See"** poem: November 30, 1928. Elisabeth Stam, *Poems and Verse*, 78.

44 **Betty Scott's Surrender**: This letter to Betty's sister Beatrice from October 7, 1926, was originally published as a small promotional pamphlet after the release of *The Triumph of John and Betty Stam*.

5. TOGETHER AT MOODY

49 **"He had the bearing"**: Secretary of faculty, quoted in Taylor, *Triumph of John and Betty Stam*, 12.

49 **"He will undoubtedly"**: Faculty member prediction, Ibid.

49 **"Expect to see"**: Another prediction, Ibid.

50 **"Never shall I"**: Isaac Page, Ibid., 42. The "wonderful verses" is a reference to "The Sands of Time Are Sinking," a hymn by Anne Ross Cousin, based on quotations from the *Rutherford Letters*.

51 **"It is an amazing"**: John Stam to brother, Ibid., 19.

51 **"The Lord has"**: John Stam to Harry Stam, Ibid., 14.

52 **"John was more than"**: Elida church congregant, Ibid., 44.

52 **"The Lord knows"**: John Stam to Jacob Stam, Ibid., 18.

53 **"My Ideal"** poem: August 1, 1924. Elisabeth Stam, *Poems and Verse*, 25–26.

55 **"A million a month"**: John Stam to brother, quoted in Taylor, *Triumph of John and Betty Stam*, 47.

57 **"Lord, I give up"**: Betty Scott's prayer: July 1925.

57 **"Betty is in Philadelphia"**: John Stam diary entry, May 24, 1931. *By Life and By Death: Excerpts and Lessons from the Diary of John C. Stam* (Grand Rapids, MI: Zondervan, 1938), 20.

58 **"Since I still feel"**: John Stam letter to parents, September 23, 1931. Box 1, Folder 3, CN 449: Correspondences (1931–1934). Wheaton Archives.

59 **"When it was over"**: Isaac Page, quoted in Taylor, *Triumph of John and Betty Stam*, 51.

59 **"A Missionary's daughter"**: Betty Scott, quoted in Huizenga, *John and Betty Stam: Martyrs*, 43–44.

6. PRESSING ONWARD

61 **"Of course it fits"**: John Stam diary entry, March 20, 1932. *By Life and By Death: Excerpts and Lessons from the Diary of John C. Stam*, 26.

62 **"I won't have"**: John Stam diary entry, April 18, 1932. Ibid., 37.

62 **"It seems to me"**: John Stam diary entry, June 30, 1932. Box 1, Folder 10, CN 449: Diary (John Stam) 1932–1933. Wheaton Archives.

64 **"Have had a blessed"**: John Stam diary entry, September 22, 1932. Box 1, Folder 10, CN 449. Ibid.

64 **"When I last saw"**: John Stam quoted by Tom, Taylor, *Triumph of John and Betty Stam*, 57.

65 **John Stam's Graduation Speech**: This speech was found among the possessions of James M. Gray in Chicago after he died on September 21, 1935. Gray stepped down as president of Moody Bible Institute on November 1, 1934, but continued serving as president emeritus. A portion of the speech was first published in *The Triumph of John and Betty Stam*, so it is assumed Gray shared it with Geraldine Taylor before its first printing in June 1935. More of the speech was then published for the December 1935 issue of *Moody Monthly* magazine. A full copy of this speech can be found in Box 1, Folder 11, CN 449: John Stam Graduation Speech. Wheaton Archives.

7. JOURNEY TO CHINA

71 **"I have seen"**: John Stam letter to family members, October 13, 1932. Box 1, Folder 3, CN 449. Wheaton Archives.

72 **"Hallelujah! Wonders never"**: John Stam diary entry, October 12, 1932. Box 1, Folder 10, CN 449. Wheaton Archives.

72 **"And then everybody"**: John Stam letter to family members, October 19, 1932. Box 1, Folder 3, CN 449. Wheaton Archives.

73 **John Stam's language school schedule**: John Stam letter to family members, November 5, 1932. Ibid.

74 **"Anhwei is the flattest"**: Betty Scott letter to Kenneth Scott, quoted in Taylor, *Triumph of John and Betty Stam*, 64.

75 **"Here in this work"**: Betty Scott, Ibid., 68.

76 **"If you shoot"**: quoted in John Stam letter below.

76 **"Afraid? Of What?"**: John Stam letter to family members with "Afraid? Of What?" poem, December 24, 1932. Box 1, Folder 3, CN 449. Wheaton Archives. There is an additional verse to this poem that John did not include in his letter, which would be located between the third and fourth stanzas presented.

8. CONSECRATED COUPLE

79 **"Today one quarter"**: John Stam diary entry, January 17, 1933. Box 1, Folder 10, CN 449. Wheaton Archives.

80 **"Hallelujah! Phew, that's"**: John Stam letter to family members, March 25, 1933. Box 1, Folder 3, CN 449. Wheaton Archives.

80 **"There wasn't a suggestion"**: John Stam letter to family members, March 29, 1933. Ibid.

81 **"It is intended"**: John Stam pamphlet to supporters, March 29, 1933. Ibid.

81 **"How clearly I remember"**: George Birch letter to John Stam's parents, December 28, 1934. Box 1, Folder 5, CN 449: Correspondences, Condolences (1934–1937). Wheaton Archives.

81 **"It would be"**: John Stam letter to family members, May 15, 1933. Box 1, Folder 3, CN 449. Wheaton Archives.

82 **"On our first"**: George Birch letter to John Stam's parents, December 28, 1934. Box 1, Folder 5, CN 449. Wheaton Archives.

82 **"This is the type"**: John Stam letter to family members, May 29, 1933. Box 1, Folder 3, CN 449. Wheaton Archives.

83 **"If dirty grass"**: John Stam letter to family members, August 12, 1933. Ibid.

83 **"Was much helped"**: John Stam diary entry, October 11, 1933. Box 1, Folder 10, CN 449. Wheaton Archives.

84 **John Stam's four praises**: John Stam letter to family members, October 15, 1933. Box 1, Folder 3, CN 449: Wheaton Archives.

85 **"Everyone seemed to"**: Charles and Clara Scott note to supporters, November 11, 1933. Box 1, Folder 8, CN 449: Correspondence with Charles Ernest Scott (1933–1935). Wheaton Archives.

85 **"Despite our fears"**: John Stam letter to family members, October 31, 1933. Box 1, Folder 3, CN 449. Wheaton Archives.

85 **"I wish I could describe"**: Ibid.

86 **"To John, from Betty"** poem: Date written unknown, but likely late 1931 or early 1932 after Betty arrived in China, Elisabeth Stam, *Poems and Verse*, 123.

9. SERVING AS ONE

87 **"John is out"**: Betty Stam letter to John Stam's parents, December 10, 1933. Ibid.

88 **"Ancestor worship with"**: John Stam letter to family members, March 5, 1934. Ibid.

89 **"We have enjoyed"**: Betty Stam letter to John Stam's parents, February 16, 1934. Ibid.

90 **"How can one"**: Mrs. Wang quoted from John Stam in letter to family members, June 4, 1934. Ibid.

91 **"Mrs. Wang's home"**: John Stam letter to family members, June 4, 1934. Ibid.

10. HELEN PRISCILLA

93 **"I'm very glad now"**: John Stam letter to family members, July 18, 1934. Box 1, Folder 3, CN 449. Wheaton Archives.

93 **"I'm glad I'm not"**: John Stam letter to family members, August 2, 1934. Ibid.

94 **"Incidentally, they want"**: John Stam letter to family members, September 8, 1934. Ibid.

95 **"The baby looks like"**: Betty Stam letter to John Stam's parents, October 22, 1934. Ibid.

96 **"Oh, no, no!"**: Mr. Peng dialogue quoted from deposition by William Hanna before George Atcheson Jr., Consul of the United States of America, in and for the consular district of Nanking, China, January 1, 1935. Box 1, Folder 7, CN 449. Wheaton Archives.

97 **"It was very"**: John Stam letter to family members, November 19, 1934. Box 1, Folder 3, CN 449. Wheaton Archives.

11. BY LIFE OR BY DEATH

99 **"I have opened"**: John Stam letter to family members, December 5, 1934. Ibid.

100 **"Rumors are around"**: John Stam's last diary entry, December 5, 1934. *By Life and By Death: Excerpts and Lessons from the Diary of John C. Stam*, 60.

100 **"Then it's your life"**: Soldier and man dialogue, Taylor, *Triumph of John and Betty Stam*, 104. The details surrounding the death of this unknown prisoner were shared in Suancheng by the wife of a Chinese witness to the Stams' murder with William Hanna in late December 1934. This event in the Stam story has endured debate over exactly what date and location this sacrifice took place, if at all. William Hanna testified that he had no reason to doubt the woman's claim, but a few early 1935 documents suggest she told Hanna the sacrifice took place in Miaosheo after John and Betty's murders. I have chosen to present the location as Tsingteh due to the two earliest full-length books of their lives having it as such, as well as out of respect to their being written with the permission of both families.

101 **"Where are you going?"**: Postmaster and John Stam dialogue, Taylor, *Triumph of John and Betty Stam*, 104.

101 **John Stam letter to CIM officials**: December 7, 1934. "His Witnesses Unto Death: A Tribute to John and Elisabeth Stam," 26. *China's Millions*: Vol. 42, No. 2, February 1935. Box 1, Folder 1, CN 449: Articles and Clippings (1935–1940). Wheaton Archives.

12. THE MIRACULOUS RESCUE

105 **"This man is"**: Chang Hsiu-sheng dialogue, Taylor, *Triumph of John and Betty Stam*, 111. Also taken from "John and Betty Stam In Memoriam" pamphlet, 6. Box 1, Folder 1, CN 449. Wheaton Archives.

107 **Two Chinese five-dollar bills**: Some early documents and articles say Pastor Lo found a Chinese $10 bill instead of two $5 bills. I chose to present it in this book as the latter due to most family members and recognized published material recalling it as such.

108 **"You have seen"**: Pastor Lo addressing crowd quoted from George Birch in letter to John Stam's parents, December 28, 1934. Box 1, Folder 5, CN 449. Wheaton Archives.

108 **"Personally I have not"**: George Birch letter to John Stam's parents, December 28, 1934. Ibid.

109 **"This is all we"**: Mrs. Lo to George Birch, quoted in Taylor, *Triumph of John and Betty Stam*, 115.

110 **"After Helen's Rescue"**: Ray Smith, Correspondence with author, March 2023.

111 **"I am so anxious"**: Lois Walton, quoted in Taylor, *Triumph of John and Betty Stam*, 116.

112 **"Open My Eyes"** poem: December 1, 1928. Elisabeth Stam, *Poems and Verse*, 79.

13. GLOBAL IMPACT

113 **"We know that"**: Cornelius Stam, "Survivors Hide Their Grief in Faith." *The Paterson Evening News*: December 13, 1934.

114 **"Our dear children"**: Peter Stam, quoted in Huizenga, *John and Betty Stam: Martyrs*, 91–93.

115 **"Oh, why did they"**: Lady and Peter Stam dialogue, Taylor, *Triumph of John and Betty Stam*, 124.

115 **"As my father"**: Jack Vinson's son, Ibid.

116 **"When the telegram"**: Clara Scott letter to Nathan and Lois Walton, December 15, 1934. "John and Betty Stam In Memoriam" pamphlet, 14. Box 1, Folder 1, CN 449. Wheaton Archives.

116 **"To me, it is"**: Clara Scott letter to Nathan and Lois Walton, December 15, 1934. Ibid., 15.

117 **"Many people would"**: Kenneth Scott, quoted in Taylor, *Triumph of John and Betty Stam*, 122–123.

117 **"When our Chinese"**: Grace Birch letter to John Stam's parents, December 27, 1934. Box 1, Folder 5, CN 449. Wheaton Archives.

118 **"When the coffins were"**: Gordon Dunn, "For the Stams No Deliverance." *East Asia's Millions*: November/December 1984.

119 **"We thank God for"**: William Hanna, quoted in Taylor, *Triumph of John and Betty Stam*, 125.

119 **"We all go Home"**: Missionary's letter to Betty Stam's parents, Ibid., 121.

119 **"They illustrate Paul's"**: Charles Scott, Ibid., 128–129.

119 **"Two of our splendid"**: Will H. Houghton, quoted in Huizenga, *John and Betty Stam: Martyrs*, 87.

120 **"It is needless"**: James M. Gray, quoted in Taylor, *Triumph of John and Betty Stam*, 120.

121 **"I am a new"**: Chinese woman in Nanking, quoted in Clara and Charles Ernest Scott, "In Loving Memory," 42. Box 1, File 1:3. Princeton Archives.

121 **"The papers everywhere"**: Lewis Sperry Chafer, quoted in Clara and Charles Ernest Scott, "In Loving Memory," 74: Box 1, File 1:3. Princeton Archives.

121 **"There is no more"**: Walter Lingle, "Talks on Timely Topics: Our Missionary Martyrs," *Christian Observer*: February 27, 1935: Box 1, File 1:3. Princeton Archives.

121 **"We can only rejoice"**: Robert Speer, quoted in Clara and Charles Ernest Scott, "In Loving Memory," 30: Box 1, File 1:3. Princeton Archives.

122 **"Nearly one hundred"**: Methodist pastor, Ibid., 33.

122 **"Will you please tell"**: Little girl in London church, Ibid.

123 **"It has been"**: "His Witnesses unto Death: A Tribute to John and Elisabeth Stam," 25. *China's Millions*: Vol. 43, No. 2, February 1935. Box 1, Folder 1, CN 449. Wheaton Archives.

124 **"CHINA: Undercurrent of Joy,"** *TIME*, December 24, 1934, 20. Used under license, reproduced by permission.

14. LEGACY

128 **"My father was"**: Cheryl Brodersen, Correspondence with author, August 2022.

128 **"Every time I read"**: (Two sources combined) John Piper, *This Momentary Marriage: A Parable of Permanence* (Wheaton, IL: Crossway, 2009), 14. John Piper, "Alone on Sunday Night," *Bethlehem Star Newsletter*: June 11, 1984. Used with permission by John Piper. Correspondence with author, July 2022.

128 **"As I turned"**: John W. Peterson, *The Miracle Goes On* (Grand Rapids, MI: Zondervan, 1976), 73–75.

129 **"My dad founded"**: Wayne Kirkpatrick, Correspondence with author, August 2023.

129 **"The legacy of"**: Keith and Kristyn Getty, Correspondence with author, October 2023.

130 **"When I taught"**: Erwin Lutzer, Correspondence with author, June 2023.

130 **"The whole Graham family"**: Ruth Graham on behalf of siblings, Correspondence with author, February 2023.

131 **"John believed God"**: Art Birch, Correspondence with author, March 2022.

EPILOGUE: A NOTE FROM THE AUTHOR

136 **"Finally I simply"**: Cornelius Stam, *Memoirs*, 79.

SUBJECT INDEX

Peterson, John W., 128–129
Piper, John, 128
Pius XI (Pope), 35
Porteous, Mr. and Mrs. R. W., 51

R

Rachmaninoff, Sergei, 27
ransom, process of, 50–51
Red Army (China), 15–16, 50, 100–103, 105, 106, 111
RMS *Empress of Japan,* 71
Rodgers, Nancy, 73, 84

S

Schoerner, Otto, 136
Scott, Beatrice (Bunny), 32, 41, 44–47, 95, 139
Scott, Charles Ernest, 31, 32–37, 42, 57, 71, 76, 85, 111, 116, 119, 122, 139
Scott, Clara Emily Heywood, 31, 32–37, 57, 85, 90, 95, 111, 116–117, 122, 130, 139
Scott, Francis (Laddie), 32, 139
Scott, Helen, 32, 37, 139
Scott, Kenneth (Ken), 32, 74, 117, 139
Shandong Province, 32, 138
Shanghai, 17, 63, 64, 71–73, 84, 85, 101–103, 109, 122, 138
Shanghai Massacre, 50
Smith, Cheryl, 128
Smith, Chuck, 128
Smith, Gertrude, 110
Smith, Howard, 110
Smith, Ray, 110
Speer, Elliot, 121–122
Speer, Robert, 121–122
Stam, Amelia Elisabeth Alletta Williams, 21–22, 23–24, 27, 113, 139
Stam, Amelia G., 139
Stam, Betty
  background of, 31–37
  burial of, 107–108, 117–118
  capture of, 100–103
  challenges of, 42, 63–64, 74
  characteristics of, 41, 43
  as consecrated couple, 79–86
  death of, 103
  education of, 35, 37, 39, 40–42, 61
  engagement of, 72
  global impact of, 113–125

You finished reading!

Did this book help you in some way? If so, please consider writing an honest review wherever you purchase your books. Your review gets this book into the hands of more readers and helps us continue to create biblically faithful resources.

Moody Publishers books help fund the training of students for ministry around the world.

The **Moody Bible Institute** is one of the most well-known Christian institutions in the world, training thousands of young people to faithfully serve Christ wherever He calls them. And when you buy and read a book from Moody Publishers, you're helping make that vital ministry training possible.

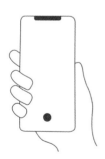

Continue to dive into the Word, *anytime, anywhere.*

Find what you need to take your next step in your walk with Christ: from uplifting music to sound preaching, our programs are designed to help you right when you need it.

Download the **Moody Radio App** and start listening today!